Journeying In His Light

Rev. William A. Anderson, D. Min.

Religious Education Division
Wm. C. Brown Company Publishers
Dubuque, Iowa

Book Team

Publisher—Ernest T. Nedder
Editorial Director—Sandra Hirstein
Production Editor—Marilyn Bowers Gorun
Production Coordinator—Marilyn Rothenberger
Art Director—Cathy Frantz

ISBN 0–697–02243–9

10   9   8   7   6   5   4   3   2   1

CONTENTS

Introduction

A friend of mine had dedicated his life to caring for his two crippled parents. For as long as I could remember, he would always leave any gathering early to get home "to the folks." Shortly after this man turned thirty, his mother died. His father, broken in spirit, followed her in death less than a month later. At the age of thirty, this friend found his life empty. He had given every extra hour to his parents to keep them out of a nursing home. He now decided that he had to "get away" "to get his head together." His journey for the next five years took him through many different jobs in many different places. When he returned home to the neighborhood, he had a story to tell about the journeys which took place outside himself and within himself. His story was one of dedication, sacrifice, goodness, frustration, anger, despair, and finally success. He had married and found the fresh flow of life he needed in his new family.

Our story is also a journey that wanders through many of the emotions felt by this friend. This formation guide is meant to be an opportunity to reflect on our story in light of the Scriptures. In fact, the journey we are about to begin should be a major part of our personal story.

FORMATION

We actually form ourselves from within. No one is able to pour formation into us as though she or he were filling an empty glass with water. Formation consists in testing our own experiences and conclusions against those of others. It could also consist in stating for ourselves our feelings and our experiences. We often forget to take time to listen to ourselves.

THE FIRST JOURNEY: *IN HIS LIGHT*

Journeying In His Light follows on a companion book entitled *In His Light*. Some who used *In His Light* for religious instructions within the parish sought a book for reflection and prayer which would draw extensively on the Scriptures and personal experience. *In His Light* offers instructions for the RCIA process, for adult and high school education, for teacher training, and for a multitude of other programs which seek to present the Christian message in nontechnical language. *Journeying In His Light* offers a book which may be used with *In His Light* (see schema at the end of this section), or used by itself with groups or privately to attain some personal goals.

ARRANGEMENT OF *JOURNEYING IN HIS LIGHT*

Sessions

Each topic has an unnumbered session and a place for the date. This will enable the individual or group using the guide to decide on the order of the topics and the amount of time spent on each session. Some may wish to spend two or three sessions on a certain topic. In this way, the guide becomes a process rather than a set program.

Present Arrangement

The present arrangement borrows some ideas from the RCIA process and can be used during the Precatechumenate, the Catechumenate, the Enlightenment Period, and the Mystagogia.
   a. The first five topics give an opportunity for reflection on the Gospels and ones response to the Scriptures.
   b. The next group of sessions follow the chapters of the book *In His Light* and may be used with *In His Light*.
   c. Reflections on the Sundays of Lent follow on these sessions with private reflections for Holy Thursday, Good Friday, and Easter Sunday.
   d. The last sessions in the book treat themes from the Easter Season, the theme of the second coming of Christ, and the celebration of Pentecost.

SESSION ARRANGEMENT

Introduction

An introduction to each session helps set the direction of the theme under consideration. This introduction consists of a story or a short reflection on life.

Scripture Reflection

A series of three Scripture references with a short reflection follow the introduction. These Scripture references are not written out, thus enabling the reader to become more familiar with using the Bible. At times, the reader may wish to read the entire text surrounding the verses chosen for reflection. The short reflection given after the Scripture reference is meant to help the reader in his or her reflection. The reflection itself, however, should touch the individual story of each reader.

After each reflection, a question is added to help the reader in his or her response. If a reader wishes to ignore the question to express some other ideas he or she found in the text, the reader should feel free to share whatever is personally significant in the text.

Response

After the Scripture reflections, space is given for personal response. Through this response, the reader makes a decision about the reflections given throughout the chapter. Rather than simply reflecting on the manner in which the Scriptures touch our life, the response challenges us to decide how we will live our Christian life in light of these reflections.

Further Discussion

The reader will find several questions for further discussion given at the end of each session. Because little space is provided for responses to these questions, the reader may wish to use a notebook to jot down some responses to these questions before discussing them in the group.

Prayer

Except for the final sessions, a simple prayer ends each chapter. By the time the reader comes to the topics at the end of this book, he or she should be able to compose a simple prayer for himself or herself. The prayers in the book offer examples of simple and direct prayers which will serve as a model for the reader to compose his or her personal prayers at the end.

SUGGESTED USES FOR *JOURNEYING IN HIS LIGHT*

A book of this type offers itself to many different and creative uses. The list given here touches many areas in which the book may be used, yet some will find other uses not mentioned here. This list will hopefully help many to use the book in some new and creative way on their spiritual journey.

RCIA

The guide follows the outline of a process for the RCIA and it is most useful for this process. Before making use of the companion book, *In His Light*, in the RCIA process, this book offers several weeks of story sharing which enables the group to become better acquainted with each other and more comfortable with sharing their questions and personal stories with one another. The freedom of choosing the number of sessions one wishes to use for each topic allows the RCIA to remain faithful to its open-ended process.

Adult Instruction

The guide enables adults to reflect on their Christian faith. Not only do they learn, but they are able to apply their learning to life. As a companion to *In His Light*, the book will be even more helpful in making this application of one's learning to one's life as a Christian.

Discussion Groups

The guide enables the members of the discussion group to share the reflections of their own story and the Scriptures with one another, while at the same time offering opportunities for discussing the lessons treated in the book *In His Light.*

High School Classes

This guide challenges the student to become more involved in class discussion. It would be even more helpful where the class could break down into groups and a secretary for each group could report the results of the reflections to the class.

Confirmation Programs

At a time when the youth of the parish are becoming more aware of their need to express their faith, this book offers an opportunity for the teacher or leader to encourage the students to reflect on the Scriptures and to share their reflections with others. It will be helpful as a later reminder to the student of the reflections which took place during the period of confirmation preparation.

Teacher Training

This book will enable teachers to learn and, at the same time, to share their reflections with one another. It could also be used for a portion of the teachers' meetings, thus setting the tone for the meeting and allowing the teachers to encourage and support one another through their reflections.

Parish Renewal

The book enables the parish to enter into a renewal at the same time the RCIA is in process, or at the time of an intensive parish renewal program. If a parish mission or short term renewal is taking place, the book could be used for discussion during the renewal period and the pastor could invite the parishioners to continue the renewal throughout the year through reflection groups. In this way, the renewal or mission would have a long-term effect upon the parish.

Spiritual Direction

This book offers opportunities for spiritual companions to help each other on their spiritual journey. And it will enable a spiritual director to know more about the one seeking direction if he or she has some personal reflections to share.

Family Prayer and Reflection

For families who wish to pray and reflect together, the book offers a format for sharing and prayer. It will enable families to discover the Scriptures together and to share their responses to the Scriptures. When this book is used by a family, parents will not only be telling their children about the faith, but they will be teaching them to be willing to share their faith and insights with others. Many parents seek ways of being involved in the spiritual formation of their children. This book offers a means for such involvement.

Prayer Groups

Reflection on the Scriptures plays a central role in prayer groups. Through the use of this book, groups can help each other in their spiritual growth and can encourage each other to continue their personal reflections on the presence of God in their lives.

Private Prayer

This book provides an individual with a series of topics which could be used for a personal journal. It enables a person to use the book for retreats, for days of recollection, for a short period of prayer and reflection, or for daily personal growth.

YOUR GUIDE

A guide such as this takes many hours of preparation and many hours spent in correcting and improving the manuscript. I would like to thank Sister Anne Francis Bartus, SSJ, who has spent many hours reading the manuscript, and who has proven to be an insightful, honest, and most helpful critic with her many theological and scriptural insights. I would like to thank Sister Immaculate Spires, SSJ, and Sister Mary Grace Freeman, SSJ, for the time spent in correcting and proofreading the manuscript. I am also grateful to Father Gary Naegele for his suggestions for this second edition. I am especially grateful to him for his suggestion that I include all three cycles of readings for the Lenten Season. I feel that this will be helpful for those who wish to use the book for Lenten reflections and for those involved in the RCIA process.

But, this is your guide and I have produced only the outline. When you finish using it, it will be your book, a written testimony of your spiritual journey. As you begin, I thank you for bringing this guide to life and for being willing to make it YOUR *Journey In His Light*.

USING *JOURNEYING IN HIS LIGHT* WITH *IN HIS LIGHT*

For those using *In His Light* and *Journeying in His Light* for the RCIA process, the following schema might prove helpful. It lists those chapters where these two books parallel each other.

———————————— Precatechumenate ————————————

In His Light	Journeying in His Light
	Topic 1 (Invitation)
	Topic 2 (Journey)
	Topic 3 (Insight—Faith)
	Topic 4 (Hope)
	Topic 5 (Love)
Chapter 1 (God)	Topic 6 (God)
Chapter 2 (Knowing God Better—O.T.)	Topics 7 and 8 (Knowing God Better—O.T.)
Chapter 3 (Jesus)	Topics 9 and 10 (Jesus)
Chapter 4 (Holy Spirit)	Topic 11 (Holy Spirit)
Chapter 5 (Sin and Life)	Topic 12 (Sin and Life)

The Invitation

INTRODUCTION

Life is filled with invitations! Over the past year, you have most likely received an invitation to a birthday party, a wedding, or a dinner at the home of a friend. Some of the invitations you have accepted while others you have politely rejected.

Besides these simple invitations, some people have received invitations to set out on a new way of life. The couple who entered marriage, the man ordained to the priesthood, the woman who accepted the call to religious life, or the person who chose to live a single life have all accepted an invitation this year.

Whenever Christ calls us, he invites us to a new way of life, even if it means only a small change in our life. Whenever we seek to know more about Christ or to draw closer to God, we are accepting an invitation. This invitation comes to us every day, sometimes in small ways, sometimes in large ways.

As we begin this session, we are accepting an invitation.

SCRIPTURE REFLECTIONS

Luke 19:1–10   *We could picture Zacchaeus moving his stacks of coins with lightning speed when someone announced that Jesus was coming. The sight of Jesus might have offered a welcome diversion to an otherwise uneventful day. Zacchaeus did not realize that Jesus was inviting himself into his life.*

During the times in which Jesus lived, a person who ate with another shared not only in that person's table, but also in that person's life. When Jesus told Zacchaeus that he would dine with him, he was telling Zacchaeus that he wanted to enter his life. Jesus was not just inviting Zacchaeus to enter his life, but even more he was inviting

9

himself to enter Zacchaeus' life. And the tax collector knew that he could not open his door to Jesus unless he closed his heart to his greed.

Zacchaeus accepted the invitation.

How Does My Response to Jesus' Invitation in My Life Compare with That of Zacchaeus?

Mark 1:16–20   According to this passage, the first disciples did not hesitate when invited to follow Jesus. Simon and Andrew were willing to leave their way of life to follow Jesus, and James and John left their families for Jesus. In this passage, Mark is telling us that the true followers of Jesus must be willing to abandon all, immediately, when Jesus invites them to follow him.

How Does My Response to the Invitation of Jesus in My Life Compare with That of the Early Disciples?

Matthew 19:16–22   *The rich man must have felt pride when he could tell Jesus how well he kept the commandments, but Jesus asked for more. He invited the young man to share in greater blessings by giving his riches to the poor and abandoning himself to Jesus as a trusting disciple. In this passage, we have an example of one who was unable to leave all for the sake of Jesus.*

How Does the Message of the Story of the Rich Young Man Compare with My Response to the Invitation of Jesus?

MY RESPONSE

In our newspapers today, we read about dedicated people who are sacrificing their lives or suffering for the sake of the message of Christ. Some have dedicated themselves to helping the poor, while others have placed themselves in danger of death to bring peace and dignity to people in need. Others have dedicated their lives to learning about their faith and living it as well as possible.

How Do I Intend to Respond to Jesus' Call to Follow Him as I Live My Daily Life?

11

FURTHER DISCUSSION

1. How well do the attitudes of the world in which we live reflect its response to the call of Jesus?

2. Who are some people who seem to have responded to the call to follow Jesus?

3. In what ways can you persuade others that they are important and that Jesus is inviting them into his life?

PRAYER

Lord, Guide of My Life,
You continually invite me into your life
as you did with the first disciples.
And you invite yourself into my life
as you did with Zacchaeus. . . .
Guide me in rejecting the invitation of my own greed
and in accepting—immediately and fully—
your Invitation. . . .
AMEN.

The Journey

INTRODUCTION

Someone once said that a journey of many miles must begin with the first step. When we set out on a summer vacation or to a new job location, we begin a journey that will cover not only miles, but also relationships between people and even between people and God. We meet new friends, deepen our love with the friends we know, enter new mysteries, tragedies, joys, and discoveries. A journey begins not only with a first movement of a foot, but with a movement of the heart. When we commit ourselves to love, to hate, to discovery, or to an ideal, we begin a journey. When the first astronaut stepped onto the moon, he observed that this small step for a human being would be a giant leap for all people on earth. He did not mean that more people would be traveling to the moon. He meant that a journey into the future had begun and that new discoveries and a new understanding of God's creation lay at the doorstep, awaiting the beginning of a new journey.

The message of Jesus is the message of a journey. He invites his disciples to share in the journey, but he warns them of the sufferings which will mark it. Despite the sufferings, he offers new life, a new joy, and a new understanding. We too are invited to share in the journey.

SCRIPTURE REFLECTIONS

John 1:29–39   *When the disciples approached Jesus to ask where he lived, they were asking Jesus if he would accept them as disciples. Jesus' response was an invitation to join him on a journey. When Jesus said, "Come and see," he was not simply inviting them to look at his home and its furnishings. He was inviting them to join him on his journey, to come, see, and learn from him.*

What Does This Scripture Passage Say about the Attitude I Must Have to Journey through Life with Jesus?

Mark 1:32–39   *Jesus was healing those who had many afflictions, and the crowd must have been ecstatic with this new miracle worker. They swarmed to him, praised him, loved him. And in the midst of it all, Jesus drew aside to pray. This is where the excited disciples found him. They apparently were enjoying this sudden fame. They reminded Jesus that the crowd was looking for him, but Jesus in the midst of his prayer, reminded them of his journey. It would be nice to stay and enjoy the acclaim of the crowd, but he came to share the good news. This was his journey and, through his prayer, he remembered it.*

How Does Prayer Help Me to Understand My Journey with Christ?

Luke 9:51–62   *The second half of Luke's Gospel speaks of Jesus' long journey toward Jerusalem. During this journey, Jesus taught his disciples that he did not come to destroy, but to build and save. The Samaritans who rejected Jesus were as important to him as his disciples. The journey is a time of commitment, a time to leave all to follow Jesus. As Jesus heads toward his passion, death, and resurrection, he asks others to commit themselves fully to their journey with him.*

What Does This Scripture Passage Say Concerning My Journey through Life as a Companion of Jesus?

MY RESPONSE

Someone once said that it was easier to die for Christ than to live for Christ. We are often prepared to live heroic moments rather than live heroic lives. When a friend becomes critically ill, we are willing to visit that friend, to help the family, and to serve in whatever manner we can. As the sickness drags on or the friend returns home, we often grow weary and begin to forget about our dedication or thoughtfulness. The heroic moment has passed, and we are now invited to live a heroic daily life. This is difficult.

How Do I Intend to Remain Conscious of Jesus' Presence as I Continue My Journey through Life?

FURTHER DISCUSSION

1. Can you find any evidence which shows that people are conscious of the presence of Jesus during their journey?

2. How does our journey with Christ affect the lives of others?

3. Can you find any evidence in life that Jesus is still present with people in the world as they journey through life?

PRAYER

Lord, God of My Journey,
You journey with us
ahead of us
beside us. . . .
You journey as a pilgrim on earth . . .
always concerned for others
rarely resting
always supporting. . . .
Allow us to follow in your footsteps
to rest with you
and always to know you are with us.
Lord, help us always to discover
where you are staying!
AMEN.

The Insight

INTRODUCTION

A man who had dedicated most of his life to aiding persons who are disabled told of his first uncomfortable moments of mixing with these men and women. He admitted that he was the one who was disabled in his nervous attitude toward such people. A young blind girl had encouraged him to tell her his problem, and he told of his discomfort and feeling of helplessness. He ended by saying to the blind girl, "Do you *see* what I mean?" Immediately he spluttered an apology when he realized what he had just said. "Yes," she answered, "I *see* your problem better than you do." With these simple words, the man realized that the disabled have learned to live with their disability better than others could live with it. He could now *see* how they looked at life.

We use the word *see* to describe the ability to note with our eyes, and, in another way, to describe the ability to understand something or have insight into something. This insight is at the base of all our humanness. We cannot see love with our eyes, but we see love through actions, feelings, touching, and such events as time spent together. We even use the expression, "There's more to this than meets the eye." For our humanness, insight is more important than eyesight. We call our insight into the person and message of Jesus by the name *Faith.*

SCRIPTURE REFLECTIONS

Matthew 6:19–25   *Jesus calls his followers to a proper view of life. He tells them to trust God and not to allow the world to become the shaper of their attitudes. A heavenly treasure of good deeds and love for others deserves more of our energy than continuous planning for security in life. Jesus does not tell us to avoid all planning, but he warns against an over-concern for worldly goods. Our attitude* toward the world and its goods will determine whether we are viewing life through the dark lenses of the world or the bright lenses of Christ's message.

What Is My Attitude toward the Treasures of the World?

Mark 8:22–25   A blind man gains his sight . . . gradually. Our growth in faith is also gradual. As we learn more about Jesus and reflect on this knowledge, our faith deepens and we are able to see the reality of God's creation a little more clearly. Jesus is always ready to help us and to heal our spiritual vision, as he did with the blind man, but he expects us to tell him our needs as the blind man did.

What Does This Story of the Healing of the Blind Man Reveal to Me about My Growth in Faith?

Luke 24:13–35   *The two disciples on the road to Emmaus thought they had to explain Jesus' death to the stranger. But the stranger, who was Jesus, taught them instead. Luke tells us the disciples later recognized him "in the breaking of the bread." It was then that they said to one another, "Were not our hearts burning within us as he spoke to us on the way?" Their supper with the Lord and their reflection on the words of Jesus enabled the disciples to experience a new and deeper faith in their lives.*

What Message for My Life Can I Learn from the Journey of Jesus and the Disciples on the Road to Emmaus?

MY RESPONSE

People of faith change the world. Faith drives some to a life of prayer, others to a life of complete commitment to the poor, others to acts of concern or love within neighborhoods and still others to trust when all hope seems lost. Because we believe that the unseen world of God's presence and guidance is always with us, we withstand many disappointments, frustrations, and critical losses which would cripple people who lacked faith. Faith is the drive behind the acts of love and concern found in a Christian life; we always have room to grow in faith.

How Do I Intend to Make Faith More Central to My Daily Life?

FURTHER DISCUSSION

1. How does faith help you in your response to the joys and difficulties in your life?

2. What are some examples of people you know who obviously lived their lives with a strong faith?

3. Are you satisfied with the manner in which your relatives, friends, and business associates live their faith in their daily lives?

PRAYER

Lord, Giver of Light,
you open our eyes slowly
to know you
and believe in you.
Teach us to continue to believe
and help us in our unbelief.
AMEN.

The Hope

INTRODUCTION

When some of the survivors from the concentration camps of the Second World War were questioned about their spirit of survival, many of them used the word *hope* in their statements. "I had hope that my wife and family were still alive;" "I kept up hope that each day would be the day of freedom;" "I just hoped that God would keep me alive to help the other prisoners;" "God seemed to give me new hope each day." As we look at men and women such as these and look at the survival of so many people in similar circumstances through history, we can better understand the meaning of the slogan, "Hope springs eternal."

The message of Jesus is a living message of hope. How could Jesus, a rejected preacher in a land as small as Palestine, possibly hope to influence the whole world? If we were to bring salvation to the world and wanted everyone to know about it, we might have flashed it across the sky, moving the sun, moon, and stars to prove our point. But from Jesus, we learn a new meaning for hope. Even our small actions, as Jesus' actions, can bring about great results if God is with us.

SCRIPTURE REFLECTIONS

Matthew 6:26–34   *In this passage, Jesus does not tell us to sit back and let God wait on us hand and foot. He is telling us to live our faith and to have hope in God. There are some people filled with anxiety over material needs and desires. The continual bombardment from commercials makes us feel a need for comfort and fulfillment in material goods. Hope makes God the goal of our lives. We seek to serve God because we trust in God. We put our hope in God.*

How Does Trusting God Give Me Hope?

Luke 1:5–24   *Elizabeth and Zechariah were advanced in years. They should have lost all hope of having a child, but they kept praying. God granted them not only a child, but a special child—John the Baptizer. The story gives us an example of hoping against all odds, trusting that God will answer our hope.*

What Does the Story of Elizabeth and Zechariah Teach Me about Hope?

Romans 5:1–11   *In this passage, Paul tells us that faith in Jesus leads to hope. Paul loves to boast about Jesus and Jesus' concern for all people. Paul's hope rests in the fact that Jesus died for the human family when sin had a firm grip on the world. This too is our hope, namely Jesus' willingness to lay down his life for us. Jesus gives us hope.*

What Part Does Hope Play in My Life?

MY RESPONSE

Some people seem to be eternal optimists and others eternal pessimists. Unfortunately, we often label the pessimist as a "realist" and the optimist as a "dreamer." The virtue of hope reminds us that God is with us in this world and that, with God's help, we can move mountains. The person who believes that the impossible can happen very often seems to make it happen. Hope gives life, and people of hope, because they believe the impossible can happen, are often the lively, creative, and energetic people of the world.

How Do I Intend to Allow the Virtue of Hope to Influence My Attitudes toward Life?

FURTHER DISCUSSION

1. Can we still "hope" for peace in the world?

2. Do you think the attitudes of the people you know and meet are hopeful attitudes?

3. How does hope help you in your attitudes toward life?

PRAYER

Lord, Our Life and Hope,
you gave your life
that we might have life.
Fill us with the hope
that flows from your life,
that we might share with others
the spirit of your life
and the gift of hope.
AMEN.

The Wonders of Love

INTRODUCTION

A psychologist once wrote that all of us have to love and be loved and must feel worthwhile in order to survive. With love, a person can survive even in the face of overwhelming difficulties. Without love, a person's life wastes away, and daily life becomes boring and empty. A person who loves and is loved will continue to struggle against all odds; the person who is not loved and who does not love will seek death, often through suicide. We need love, and we need to experience that love in order to continue as normal human beings.

The ability to love resides within each one of us. Someone does not add love to us, but draws it out of us. When someone tells us that he or she loves us, it leaves us free to trust that person with our love. As we express that love, we discover more about love and more about ourselves.

Love does not prove itself in the tingle of an attraction to another person, but proves itself at those moments when the attraction has given way to daily dedication and commitment. Love carries us through those dry moments of life, and the moments of difficulty and boredom with another. True love shows itself in giving as well as in receiving.

God is love, and God's presence and love are at the root of our humanness. Without a moment's hesitation, we can say that love is God's most important gift to human beings.

SCRIPTURE REFLECTIONS

Mark 12:28–34   *When we study our needs, it is not surprising that Jesus would place love on the pedestal as the greatest commandment. We are a loving people who share in the love of God. We must reach the fullness of our human* calling by loving God and one another. This passage leaves us with a rare moment in the Gospels. A moment when Jesus actually praises a scribe for his insight. When we love God and our brothers and sisters, we are indeed not far from the reign of God. In fact, when we truly love, we are living in the realm of God.

What Makes Me Believe That I Am Loved and That I Love Others Well?

1 Corinthians 13:1–13   After reading this passage, we can simply ask, "What more could be said about love?" In a powerful and beautiful manner, Paul the apostle tells us that all gifts are useless without love. Love enables us to endure all, and though all else cease in life, love will continue to hold strong. In fact, of the three great virtues that will endure, faith, hope, and love, love is the greatest. This passage on love from Paul is a work of art that understands creation at its very base.

How Does My Love Affect Every Area of My Life?

1 John 4:7–21   *The reason we should love is that love comes from God and love leads to a deeper relationship with God. God is Love, and this Love loves us, not for some good actions we performed, but simply because we exist. It is not our love for God which is most amazing, but it is God's love for us. God's love for us calls us to return our love to God. Only we can give "our love" to God. God does not force us to love in return. "Our love" is our gift to God who is Love.*

How Has God's Love for Me Helped Me to Respond in Love for God?

MY RESPONSE

A famous song tells us, "What the world needs now is love, sweet love." Building on faith and hope, we now come to the greatest of the virtues, love. In order to be totally human, we must love. This includes love of God, love of self, and love of one another. Anyone who claims to love God must love his or her neighbor and have a concern for the needs of all in the world. The more we love, the closer we are to God, and the nearer we are to our total fulfillment as a human person created by God.

How Do I Intend to Make Love of God, Self, and Neighbor Even More Central to My Life in the Future?

FURTHER DISCUSSION

1. Do you think that we have lost the true meaning of love in our world today?

2. What makes people act without love?

3. Can you give any examples of people who were able to help others because they loved them?

PRAYER

Lord, Loving God,
you have come into our lives
as LOVE
and have completely shared yourself with us.
Teach to make your love
the real love of our lives
that we may love you . . .
and our sisters and brothers . . .
as ourselves.
AMEN.

In Search of God
(In His Light—Chapter One)

INTRODUCTION

There is a story of an oyster that kept covering an irritating piece of sand in its shell with a smooth substance. The oyster's trouble resulted in a very valuable pearl.

The thought of God is like a piece of sand. We cannot get away from God. Some try to dislodge God from their lives while others cradle God in the faith of their life and produce a pearl of great value. God has been in the minds and hearts of peoples and nations for centuries. Those who have tried to deny God's existence are, for the most part, forgotten.

Some people have the ability to see God in the tragedies as well as in the joys of life. The woman in the opening story to this chapter (In the book, *In His Light*—page 3) was able to see beauty in a gnarled piece of wood. In the same way, some people can see the beauty of God in all that happens in their lives.

In this chapter, we discover God through God's dealings in our daily life. God is a concerned God who touches us with this concern and who can be touched in turn through prayer. A person of faith can look to the experiences of the world and of life and find the logic of God. God certainly gives meaning to our life.

SCRIPTURE REFLECTIONS

Exodus 3:1–14   *In these short verses, the book of Exodus tells us a great deal about God. God is greater than the ancestors of Moses, namely Abraham, Isaac, and Jacob. The one God is a compassionate God, concerned for a people now in slavery. The one God is a powerful God, ready to overcome the great power of the Egyptians, and to lead the chosen people to a land, rich in the goods of the earth. God* can call anyone to service, even the self-proclaimed weak man, Moses.

The writer of these lines defines God for us, not through a dry definition, but through an episode in the life of Moses.

How Would I Define God in Terms of My Own Life?

Psalm 93   The psalms were the prayed faith of the Israelites. Their beliefs became the source of their prayer. In this psalm, the writer praises the splendor of God which stands above all the splendors of the world. It proclaims that God has created all and has power over all, and it expresses these truths in a joyous and triumphant manner.

How Well Does My Prayer Express My Image of God?

Matthew 7:7–11 *God stands ready to answer our prayer. Some believe that God ignores creation, but Jesus tells us to persist in prayer, and God will respond in some way. Since Jesus knows the love of God for each one of us, he can tell us with confidence that God who loves us will respond to our prayer.*

How Does This Scripture Passage Help Me in My Prayer?

MY RESPONSE

We were made to the image and likeness of God. This means that God created us to think, judge, will, and act with a certain amount of independence. It also means that we have an eternal call to live with God. Our response to this call begins now, during our lives on earth.

How Do I Intend to Continue Living Close to God While on Earth?

FURTHER DISCUSSION

1. How would you attempt to explain to others that God exists?

2. What would you say to those who claim that God does not care what happens to us?

3. Is it wrong to become angry with God in times of suffering or frustration?

PRAYER

Lord, God of Our Life,
you shape us . . .
you know us . . .
you love us!
Help us to know you . . .
to trust you . . .
and to love you . . .
now and forever.
AMEN.

Session Number _____

Date _____

Knowing God Better— Part 1
(In His Light—Chapter Two—questions 1–9)

INTRODUCTION

In the introduction to this chapter in the book, *In His Light*, we read the story of a man who collected junk for a living. One day in a park, a young boy saw this man playing a game with his family and viewed this man in a different light. In the same way, we better understand God through the chosen people of God.

The early communities had much to share concerning God in their lives. They would sit and share stories which portrayed a deeper understanding of God. The Spirit would guide these discussions which were real revelations about God. They not only told the deep mysteries which resided in the depth of God, but they also included the revelations that God is a loving God, a concerned God, and an involved God. This, although we often forget the fact, is also revelation, because it reveals something about God.

SCRIPTURE REFLECTIONS

Genesis 1:1–2:4a   *We can understand the message of the passage more clearly when we attempt to discover the meaning of the scriptural text rather than dwell on its scientific or historical facts. God created the world out of nothing, brought order into the world, and made human beings the peak of creation. The story may not tell us how the world actually began, but it does tell us about the power of God and the importance of human beings in creation. "And God saw that it was good."*

What Does This Scripture Passage Tell Me about My Part in Creation?

Exodus 14:5–31   The Exodus is the central story of the Old Testament. God promised Abraham through a covenant that God would always be with the family of Abraham. Now the Exodus takes the Israelite slaves into the desert with the hope of reaching the promised land. The Exodus becomes a symbol of the life of all of us as we journey toward God. The Israelites followed Moses with joy; later they cursed him for leading them to destruction; then they rejoiced after crossing the sea. These will be the signs of their journey—joy, complaining, turning to God, and turning against God. Through this journey, we learn of God and how God responds to such a fickle horde of people.

How Can This Scripture Passage Help Me in My Attitude toward God's Presence in My Life?

1 Samuel 16:1–13   *God did not wish to have a king over the Israelites, but the people had insisted. The first king, Saul, had proved unworthy. Now God showed concern for the people and chose David as king. David will become the great ancestor of the Messiah. Despite his great love for God, he will still sin. David will seek forgiveness with genuine sorrow.*

What Does God's Choice of David Tell Me about My Relationship with God?

MY RESPONSE

In the Scriptures, we read about agreements made between God and leaders of the Israelites. These agreements, called *covenants*, commit the people to God and God to the people. From the moment of our baptism, we enter a similar agreement with God, an agreement by which we commit ourselves to live in union with Christ and God's people. We call this a *covenant*. It touches us at the depth of our being, at every moment of our lives. The fact that baptism is a covenant tells us the importance of this gift.

How Do I Intend to Live out My Covenant with God?

FURTHER DISCUSSION

1. How would you answer someone who asked you to explain how Cain found someone to marry?

2. How does the Exodus experience of the Israelites teach us a lesson for our own lives?

3. What are some examples of covenants in our lives and how do they differ from contracts?

PRAYER

Lord, Creator and Guide,
you prepared a universe
for your people . . .
and you asked that we use it
to honor you
and love one another. . . .
Help us, Lord, in our failures
and guide us back
to the purpose and meaning
of your creation. . . .
AMEN.

Knowing God Better— Part 2

(In His Light—Chapter Two—questions 10–12)

INTRODUCTION

God had chosen the people of Israel as special people in Old Testament times. We learn much about God by looking back to these people and their history and traditions. God not only speaks to us through the great leaders of those days, but God also speaks to us through the prophets and the other writings which give us insight into the great mystery of God.

Within families, there always seem to be some children who can best understand the wishes of the parents. The rest of their family will often contact them before making any important or minor decision concerning the parents. This seems to be the role of the prophets and the Wisdom writers. They understand God and know what God wants for the chosen people. But they suffer when they remind the family of God's expectations.

SCRIPTURE REFLECTIONS

1 Samuel 3:1–21   *Once Samuel accepted the call to be a prophet, he also discovered the cost of prophecy. As a prophet, Samuel would first tell his beloved teacher Eli that God had condemned Eli's family. Throughout his life, Samuel will plead with the people on behalf of God and will act in the name of God in anointing their first two kings. Like Samuel, modern-day prophets will experience suffering and joy when they speak and act in God's name.*

Am I Able to See My Life as Important for the Fulfillment of God's Mission on Earth?

Jeremiah 20:7–18   *Jeremiah shows us the anguish of a prophet. He complains to God, he praises God, and he ends by cursing the day he was born. Jeremiah shows us a human prophet, speaking out in the name of God, undergoing suffering for his dedication to God, and coming close to despair. Jeremiah was a great prophet, a great saint. We can look to him in our anguish over the difficulties we must face for God and see in Jeremiah an example of a struggling prophet. Once we accept the call to speak and act in the name of God, we will face misunderstandings, anguish and even anger with God. But Jeremiah reminds us that God never abandons us, and, no matter what happens, we should never abandon God.*

What Lessons for My Life Can I Learn from Jeremiah the Prophet?

Psalm 30   *In this psalm, the author gives us an example of how we should pray. He praises God for protecting him, invites others to join in this praise, expresses his experiences of fear when God seemed hidden, and finally offers praise to God for turning his sorrow into joy. This is a good example of the way in which the people of Israel experienced their faith.*

How Does My Prayer Compare with That of the Psalmist?

MY RESPONSE

To speak and act in God's name takes courage. It also demands an ability to determine whether or not we are actually fulfilling God's will or our own. All of us are prophets whenever we act or speak in the name of God. Before we can call others to share in God's life, we are first called to live that life. The messages we share as prophets are living messages which come from our hearts as well as our lips.

How Do I Intend to Fulfill My Call as a Prophet in Our Modern World?

FURTHER DISCUSSION

1. Who are some modern day prophets and how do they compare with the prophets of the Scriptures?

2. Can you identify any passages in the Wisdom Books which have special applications to our lives today?

3. How does God communicate with us today?

PRAYER

Lord, Sharer of Wisdom,
teach us to hear your Word
as you speak to us
through the Scriptures.
And guide us to find your wisdom
in these words
that we might understand you
and love you. . . .
AMEN.

Session Number _____

Date _____

Jesus Is Lord—Part 1
(In His Light—Chapter Three—questions 1–4)

INTRODUCTION

In the introduction to this chapter of the book, *In His Light*, a fisherman is saved by an unknown hero and his life changed. Into the history of the world came Jesus Christ, and the life of the world changed.

When we read about the life and message of Jesus Christ, we meet a truly amazing person. He was God, yet he came to share in our humanness because he loved us and wanted to save us. With the genius and freedom of the writing style of the day, the authors of the Gospels told us not only of the life of Jesus; they also told us who he really was—God become human. They had a new insight into the life of Jesus that developed from an understanding of his resurrection. They wove this new insight into their message and lay before the world, not a biography of Jesus, but an intimate glimpse at the person and the message of Jesus, like precious jewels polished to their true perfection under the guidance of the Holy Spirit.

SCRIPTURE REFLECTIONS

Luke 2:1–21   *The birth of Jesus challenges us to reflect on our response to the presence of Christ in our lives. Because his own people rejected him, Jesus comes into the world in the midst of poverty. The shepherds, considered sinners by the people of their day, respond to a call from God's messengers and go to worship him. Mary can only reflect on all that is happening, trying to understand the full meaning of the mystery of the birth of Jesus. Finally, the child receives the name chosen by God, the name of Jesus which recalls the saving mission of Jesus on earth.*

What Message for My Life Do I Receive from This Passage as I (Like Mary) Ponder ALL These Things in My Heart?

Matthew 21:33—46   In this parable, the chosen people of Israel are the tenants who received the call to tend the garden of God on earth. Their leaders, however, killed the prophets and eventually led the Romans to kill Jesus. For this reason, Jesus tells them that they will lose the garden and that it will be turned over to others. These are those who were not among the people of God, the people of other nations known as the Gentiles.

What Message for My Life Can I Learn from This Parable?

Mark 15:33–47   *In Jesus' passion, we view him as completely abandoned. Many who believed in Jesus up to this time now faltered in their belief, while a centurion, who had not faith up till this time, uttered, "Clearly this was the Son of God!" Some find God in strength only while others find God in the moment of complete powerlessness. A dramatic, exciting life apparently ends in the silence of a tomb behind a huge stone.*

Have I Ever Been Able to Discover Christ in Moments of Weakness?

MY RESPONSE

The message of the Gospels enables us to understand the faith of the early Church community and the faith which God calls us to live today. In many Scripture texts, we read about people who "pondered these words (or events)" in their hearts. No matter how often we ponder the words of the Gospels, we will always be making new discoveries for our lives. To profess faith in Christ, we must nourish our faith. The writings of the early Christians, called by some the Christian Scriptures (the New Testament), offer us this nourishment.

How Do I Intend to Nurture My Faith in the Future?

FURTHER DISCUSSION

1. How have the Gospels been helpful to you in the development of your faith?

2. How have the infancy narratives influenced your faith?

3. What do you find most encouraging in the life of Jesus as presented in the Gospels?

PRAYER

Lord, One with Us,

you lived within our human family,
sharing your gifts with us,
and accepting our suffering.

Give us the courage and understanding
which will allow us
to live as one with you,
sharing your gifts
with one another.

AMEN.

Session Number _____

Date _____

Jesus Is Lord—Part 2
(In His Light—Chapter Three—questions 5-10)

INTRODUCTION

A well known children's story is that of *The Prince and the Pauper.* Two boys, who looked alike, changed places and discovered what it was like to lead a life different from the lives of their younger years.

The life of Jesus is no tale. It is the story of God become human for love of us. But the impact of this humanness did not really strike some Christians until they realized the extent of Jesus' humanness. He emptied himself of his powers to become a weak, insecure human being like ourselves. It would have been a great act of love for God to become human and still retain his God powers and his God mind. But to become human and empty himself of these powers until his resurrection—this is an astounding act of love. God, the great Lover, did just that! And he did that for us paupers, that we might share his life for all eternity.

SCRIPTURE REFLECTIONS

Philippians 2:6-11   *Although Jesus was God from all eternity, he "emptied himself" and took the form of a slave. He not only became human, he also came as a weak human servant. The hymn tells us that he lived in total obedience throughout his life, and that God the Father highly exalted him so that all the world would worship him and call him their divine "Lord." Jesus had the right to be "like God" throughout his human life, but he emptied himself. The contrast reminds us of Adam who sinned to be "like God." Jesus offers us an example of true humanness through his acceptance of the "form of a servant."*

45

How Well Do I "Empty" Myself for the Service of Others?

Mark 8:27–33   When Peter glibly professed that Jesus was the Messiah, he did not fully understand what he was saying. Jesus had to pass through his passion to his resurrection. When Peter chides Jesus about his prediction of these final events, Jesus sees Peter as trying to turn Jesus away from his mission. He responds harshly to Peter, telling him, "Get out of my sight, you Satan." Peter did not realize that Jesus would bring salvation through his own death and resurrection.

What Does This Scripture Passage Tell Me about My Life as a True Disciple of Jesus?

1 Corinthians 15:20–28   *Paul explains the effect of the resurrection upon Christians. Just as one, Adam, brought sin into the world, so another, Christ, brought abundant life for all who believe in him. Christians now act in the person of Christ throughout their lives and, at the end, Christ will present all of perfected creation to God as a total gift of praise. We will be part of that gift. The world comes from God, and through Christ's death and resurrection, all will return to God.*

How Does My Sharing in the Gifts of the Resurrection of Christ Affect My Attitude Toward Life?

MY RESPONSE

As Christians, we share in the life and message of Jesus Christ. If the world is to see Christ present today, it must look to us and the way we live our lives. Christ continues to live on in us through the power of his resurrection. It is our duty to allow the world to experience this presence of Christ. Our manner of life, more than our words, gives witness to Christ in our lives.

How Do I Intend to Continue to Make the Presence of Christ Present in My Life?

FURTHER DISCUSSION

1. In what ways would you say your life is different because of the resurrection of Jesus Christ?

2. How would you describe your image of the human Jesus?

3. What are your feelings concerning the second coming of Christ?

PRAYER

Lord, Giver of Life,
you died and were raised
that we might have life.
Give us the faith needed
to die with you
and to live with the hope
of being raised with you.
AMEN.

The Holy Spirit in Our Lives

(In His Light—Chapter Four)

INTRODUCTION

Catholics today are experiencing many varied forms of worshipping God. Some are raising their hands to the heavens as they pray, singing out a joyous and loud song to the Lord. Others are speaking in tongues, hugging, and shouting out "alleluia" as someone prays over them. Others are quietly sitting in their seats, running their fingers over their rosary beads, and still others are praying and singing with the community in an orderly fashion. All profess that the Holy Spirit is guiding them in their prayer, and that it is the power of the Holy Spirit surging through them which enables them to praise God in faith.

We are living in an age which uses the word *Spirit* far more often than in the past. The awareness of the role of the Spirit in worship and in our daily lives is growing, and it lies at the root of our need to reflect upon the work of the Spirit in our lives.

SCRIPTURE REFLECTIONS

Mark 1:1–13   *John the Baptizer proclaims that a new type of baptism will take place, a baptism which is more than a commitment made with water alone. John predicts a baptism which will actually bring the Spirit into the life of a person. Lest we misunderstand the meaning of the Holy Spirit, Mark tells of the Holy Spirit coming upon Jesus and driving him out to the desert, as though he were totally possessed by the Spirit. In reality, when the awareness of* the Spirit and the love of the Spirit overtake us, we can do nothing but allow ourselves to respond to that love if we are to live a fulfilled life.

How Has the Spirit Guided Me Thus Far through Life?

John 16:5–15   *Jesus must leave this world to allow the Spirit to become even more active. The Spirit will prove the message of Jesus to be a true message from God. The logic of the world will totter under the reality of God's message as shared through the Spirit. Although Jesus has spent the years of his public life with the disciples, there are truths that they cannot even begin to understand without the help of the Spirit. With the death, resurrection, and ascension of Jesus, the Holy Spirit will come upon the disciples, and with the Spirit, a new dawning of understanding of the message of Jesus. The Spirit will continue to share with the disciples the message of Jesus.*

How Has the Holy Spirit Helped Me to Know More about God?

Acts 2:1–18   *The effects of the coming of the Holy Spirit upon the followers of Jesus drive them out of the upper room to spread the word of God. Peter tells them that the world has changed, that the prophecy of Joel (3:1–5) now takes effect. Through the gift of the Holy Spirit, we shall have prophets, visionaries, dreamers, and a hopeful group of people professing faith in Jesus Christ. The world is different because of the power of the Holy Spirit.*

Can I Say That the Holy Spirit Is Visibly at Work within Me?

My Response

The Holy Spirit helps us through difficult moments in life by giving us courage and strength. The Spirit also guides us in worship, protects us in temptation, enables us to know God, and leads us to God through life. In our lives as Christians, the Holy Spirit is always active. The activity of the Holy Spirit, however, depends on our openness to the gifts of the Spirit.

How Do I Intend to Continue to Remain Open to the Gifts of the Holy Spirit in My Life?

FURTHER DISCUSSION

1. Do you see any evidence that the Holy Spirit is at work in the world today?

2. How does a knowledge of the Holy Trinity affect your daily life?

3. What is your opinion concerning the charismatic movement in the Church today?

PRAYER

Lord, Giver of Life,
send the Spirit into our lives
that we may share our faith,
with wisdom and love.
AMEN.

Sin and Life
(In His Light—Chapter Five)

INTRODUCTION

"Jaws" was a movie about a killer shark that attacked people at a popular beach. The large shark would strike at swimming vacationers, destroying the peace and rest they had hoped to find during vacation.

The world God created could have been a wonderful world in which people lived and cared for one another. It could almost have been one large vacation, filled with loving dedication to one's responsibilities. But, like the large white shark in "Jaws," sin lurked just below the surface and eventually began to tear lives apart.

In this chapter, we study about sin and life. Like the young boy in the introduction to the chapter in the book, *In His Light*, some people, through their own selfishness or fear, cause others suffering, either because they do not care or because they seek only their own pleasures and comfort. Sin, whether alone or with others, is the great destructive force prowling about God's creation.

But in the person of Jesus, a new hope for life dawned.

SCRIPTURE REFLECTIONS

Genesis 4:1−15   *In the first eleven chapters of the first book of the Bible, we read that sin came into the world as a result of human weakness. Once the first sin entered the world (as exemplified in the sin of Adam and Eve), other sins immediately followed. When Cain sinned, he cried out to God, "Am I my brother's keeper?" Not only did Cain refuse to show concern for his brother, he even sought to destroy him. Through this story, we hear God telling us that the harm done to all people cries out to God from the soil of this world.*

Once we sin, like Cain, we too become restless wanderers on this earth.

How Does Sin Affect the Attitudes of My Daily Life?

Romans 6:1—14   Paul sees in the mystery of the resurrection of Jesus a sign of death to sin and resurrection to a new life. When we enter into union with Jesus through our baptism, we become, like Jesus, dead to sin and alive to God. If we allow sin to control us, we become a slave to sin and obedient to its enticements. We now live under grace, not under the law, and with that grace we have the power to overcome sin.

How Has Jesus Helped Me to Overcome Sin in My Life?

Luke 15:1–10   *The sinner is still a valuable person to God. In this Scripture passage, we hear about the extent of that value. If just one sinner returns, the rejoicing is overwhelming. This is God's continual love for the sinner. In the midst of our sins, we are reminded of God's great love for all sinners. The sinner need never despair after reading of this great concern of God for sinners.*

How Has the Message of God's Concern for Sinners Affected My Life?

My Response

Without the help of God in our lives, the power of sin would completely overwhelm us. God has created a good world, but the power of sin has gained a strong hold on creation. Jesus brought salvation, and the Holy Spirit brings us the gifts which flow from Christ's death and exaltation. Sin still has power, but the grace of God is even more powerful.

How Do I Intend to Use God's Gifts in Overcoming the Grip of Sin in the World?

FURTHER DISCUSSION

1. How do you understand the idea of the power of sin in the world?

2. Which actions would you call sinful?

3. How does grace work in your life?

PRAYER

Lord, Giver of New Life,
you continually offer yourself
and your love
to us in spite of our sins.

Teach us to love as you love,
to forgive as you forgive
and always to seek forgiveness.

AMEN.

Session Number _____

Date _____

Our Christian Family— Church

(In His Light—Chapter Six)

INTRODUCTION

In the second book of Maccabees (chapter 7), the story is told of a mother who watched her seven sons killed, one at a time, for their faith in God. As each son went to his death, the others encouraged and supported the one being tortured, with reminders of God's gifts for those who remained faithful. The mother, the last to die, encouraged the final son to offer his life for God. She underwent the torture of seeing her sons in terrible pain until she herself had to endure her own pain and death.

In this chapter, we look to our family, the Church. The Church, like Christ, must champion many spiritual values that are not very popular in a world dominated by sin. It began with Christ and his mother, Mary, who had to watch her son ridiculed, tortured, and killed. The Church must continue to suffer for its teachings, and the sufferings are often the same—ridicule, torture, and death. The Church must always answer with love, following the example of Christ and honoring the Mother who stands by the Church at all moments of life.

The opening story to this chapter (*In His Light*, page 83) speaks of a priest who loves the Church and who likewise loves his Methodist friends. He hopes that their love of their Church is as strong as his. His family is the Church, and he wishes to share his family with his friends.

Our outlook must include a love for our family, the Church. We must yearn to share our family with others because it is truly sharing Christ with others. In this chapter, we celebrate our Christian family—the Church.

SCRIPTURE REFLECTIONS

1 Corinthians 12:12–31   *Christ continues to minister on earth through the community of Christians. The Body of Christ fulfills this mission when all perform their particular functions according to their gifts and calling. Since the mission of the Church calls for an abundance of gifts, we should recognize that our gifts are important, and the gifts of others, although different from ours, are also important. The Body of Christ praises God most perfectly when all act as one, using the various gifts for the building up of God's reign on earth. We need each other.*

What Are My Gifts, and How Do They Help the Community?

John 21:1–19   *A community of disciples (the Church) sets out to fish. On their own, they can do nothing, but when they follow the directions of Christ, they catch an abundance of fish. Simon Peter, the leader of the group, cannot wait to speak with Jesus. Jesus challenges the love of Peter, making Peter express his love three times. Each time, Jesus is offering Peter a special role in the community, the role of the shepherd. Like Jesus, Peter must be willing to lay down his life for the flock.*

How Does This Story Apply to My Life?

John 19:25–27   *Just before he dies, Jesus places his concern for his mother Mary and his disciple John in their hands. Commentators see in the words of Jesus a symbolic gesture which tells us that Mary receives the call to be the mother of all disciples, symbolized by John. The words to John symbolically remind the disciples that Mary is their mother. This text identifies Mary as the mother of the Church.*

What Does This Text Say about My Relationship to Mary?

MY RESPONSE

The Church continues the mission of Jesus on earth. We have gifts and a call to share in that mission. This call includes our love and concern for one another, for those in need, for those who have not heard of Christ, and for our unity in worship. The concern of the early Christians for those who were suffering as well as their love for one another inspired others to join them. We share in the same call as the early Christians.

How Do I Intend to Share My Gifts with the Church Community?

FURTHER DISCUSSION

1. What does the expression "You are the Church" mean?

2. What is the mission of the Church in today's world?

3. How would you answer someone who claimed that the Catholic Church worships Mary?

PRAYER

Lord, Guide of Our Family,
you are the Church
and through our baptism,
we too become Church.
Help us always to be aware
of this great call
to make your Church
visible to the world
through us.
AMEN.

Session Number _____

Date _____

The Sacraments and Love
(In His Light — Chapter Seven)

INTRODUCTION

At a conference on the value of touching and the need for it in our lives, an orderly from a hospital for the mentally ill told of a thirteen-year-old boy who sat babbling in the hospital corridor. People would smile a cheerful "Hi" as they passed by, but the boy never responded. One day, an elderly visitor to the hospital patted the boy on the head as she passed, and he ceased his babbling for a moment to look up at the woman with a smile.

More discoveries are being made concerning the value of touch in our lives. Without touch, a baby will die. Even animals deprived of touch become neurotic. We need touch in our lives for a healthy and normal development.

When Jesus gave us the sacraments, he could have chosen to pass on the gifts through a cheerful "Hi" in our direction, but he chose, instead, to touch us. Through the sacraments, Jesus touches us at important points in our lives. In the introduction to this chapter in the book, *In His Light*, we see signs as a means of being in touch with our own feelings. Through signs, God "keeps in touch" with us in the sacraments.

SCRIPTURE REFLECTIONS

Mark 5:25–34   *A woman believes that Jesus has the power to heal her, but she also believes that she must reach out to him and touch him. When she does, she receives healing. When Jesus turns to speak with her, he reminds her (and us) that it was not merely touching, but touching with faith, that cured her.*

61

How Does This Story Help Me to Understand the Role of
Faith in the Celebration of the Sacraments?

Luke 7:11–17   *Jesus touched with compassion.*
Because Jesus himself was touched by the sadness of the
widow, Jesus touched the litter and raised the widow's son
from the dead. The fact that Jesus is God tells us that God is
touched deeply by our needs and that God will respond by
touching us in some way in return.

How Does the Compassion of Christ Help Me to Place
More Trust in the Power of the Sacraments?

Luke 7:36–50   *A sinner who recognizes her sinfulness approaches Jesus as a servant. Despite her sinfulness, she dares to touch Jesus. Jesus reminds his host that it is not sin which keeps a person from approaching him, but neglect. Jesus proclaims through a parable that, because her sins are many and her conversion deep, she will love him more than one who had only a few sins.*

What Does This Story Say about the Necessity of Love in the Celebration of the Sacraments?

MY RESPONSE

Through the sacraments, the power and love of God embraces our lives and brings us healing and power to fulfill our mission in life. The sacraments are not given only for those who are celebrating them, but for the common good. Through the gift of the sacraments. God calls us to help creation become more conscious of God's love.

How Do I Intend to "Live" the Sacraments?

FURTHER DISCUSSION

1. What symbols of love are important to you, and how do they compare with the use of symbols in the sacraments?

2. Using your own words, how would you define a sacrament?

3. How would you respond to someone who says that the Catholic use of medals and rosary beads is no different than the superstitious ornaments used by primitive tribes?

PRAYER

Lord, God of Our Life,
you have touched us
and we reach out to touch you
through our prayers
through our actions
through our lives.

Through the loving touch of your sacraments,
our feeble touch
becomes one
with your loving, powerful touch.
AMEN.

Sacraments of Initiation— Part 1—Baptism

(In His Light—Chapter Eight)

INTRODUCTION

An ancient Indian tribe had a cruel and torturous ceremony for admitting adolescent boys into manhood. Due to the tremendous pain and stress involved in the ceremony, nervous parents would begin years in advance to train the boys to control their powers of concentration so that, at will, they could distract their thoughts away from the pain.

The Church, of course, does not have a cruel and torturous ceremony of initiation, but the Church realizes the great difficulty of living Christian values in a world which strives to ridicule and reject such values. In order to prepare a person to live as a true image of Christ, the Church has established a time of preparation before one shares in the Ritual of Initiation into the Catholic Church.

The Sacraments of Initiation are Baptism, Confirmation, and Eucharist. These sacraments, ordinarily celebrated for adults at the liturgy of the Easter Vigil, enable people to make Christ more present in the world. They even carry his title, as shown in the introduction to this chapter in the book, *In His Light*, and call themselves *Christians.*

Although these Sacraments of Baptism, Confirmation, and Eucharist are more properly seen in relationship to one another as Sacraments of Initiation, we have treated each separately for the sake of taking a deeper look at the meaning of each. We look first to baptism.

SCRIPTURE REFLECTIONS

Mark 1:1–11   *When Mark begins the "gospel of Jesus Christ, the Son of God," he immediately turns his attention to John the Baptizer and the baptism of Jesus. The baptism given by John symbolizes commitment to a mission, but it does not have the full symbol of the Sacrament of Baptism given by Jesus. John tells his listeners that Jesus will baptize not only with water, he will also baptize with the Holy Spirit. Jesus commits himself to his mission by allowing John to baptize him. The voice from heaven which proclaims the greatness of Jesus comes for us, the readers, so that, in the pages ahead, we might learn of Jesus' commitment and seek to follow him whom we now know as the Son of God.*

What Can I Learn about the Meaning of My Baptism from This Scripture Passage?

Matthew 28:16–20   *Baptism brings us into a life with Jesus. His mission now becomes our mission. At our baptism, Jesus does not tell us to sit back and keep ourselves away from all temptation and sin. He sends us out. When we receive the gift of baptism, we are sent out to make disciples of all nations. The fact that Jesus has sent the Spirit to help us with this mission makes the apparently impossible become possible.*

How Does the Mission Given to Jesus' Followers Affect Me?

Acts 9:1–19   *Saul meets the Lord in a dramatic way on the road to Damascus. Jesus does not send Saul on his mission immediately, but he blinds him and forces Saul into a period of deep reflection. During this time, Saul pieces together the meaning of Christ's life and message. When Ananias comes to Saul and blesses him, Saul understands more fully. The writer describes Saul's dawning in faith by using the picture of scales falling from his eyes, a symbol of Saul's emerging from physical and spiritual blindness. Saul is now prepared for his mission of witnessing to Christ.*

What Does This Scripture Passage Tell Me of My Life as a Baptized Christian?

MY RESPONSE

Baptism calls us to share the life of Christ. Through this first Sacrament of Initiation, we become a new person and are clothed in Christ. Christ calls us to be a light in the world through which the message of Jesus can shine. Like the other sacraments, baptism does not simply offer me a nice gift for life, but it calls me to act and to fulfill my mission on earth. Through this baptism, God can say of us, "This is my beloved son (daughter) in whom I am well pleased."

How Do I Intend to Fulfill My Baptismal Commitment?

FURTHER DISCUSSION

1. In what specific ways does the Sacrament of Baptism affect your life?

2. What message do you receive from the use of water as a symbol for baptism?

3. Besides the actual moment of pouring the water or the moment of immersion, what part of the baptismal ceremony is most meaningful for you?

PRAYER

Lord, One with Us,

you give us new life
through our baptism. . . .

Never allow us to forget
the source of that new life,
your own life,
given through your passion,
death, and resurrection.

Lord, allow us to live this gift
according to your example.

AMEN.

Sacraments of Initiation— Part 2—Confirmation
(In His Light—Chapter Nine)

INTRODUCTION

A teenage boy told a group of people that he was not a good Christian because he feared going downtown to a street corner and preaching about Christ. He felt that a true Christian would witness to Christ in this manner.

As we look back through history, we discover many ways of witnessing to Christ which have brought the message of his love to others. Some have died for their faith, others have preached about their faith in the parlors of strangers or on street corners, while others have preached their faith through a life of love, worship, and kind actions. A Christian is called to share the faith, but there are varieties of ways to do this.

The Sacrament of Confirmation can most properly be understood in its relationship to the Sacraments of Initiation. At one time, many felt that the Sacrament of Confirmation was not a separate sacrament, but a continuation of the Rite of Baptism. Over the past centuries, however, the role of the Sacrament of Confirmation as a special sacrament of witness to our faith has developed.

In the opening story to this chapter (*In His Light*, page 129), we read of a little boy cupping smoke in his hand. We compared that story to our faith questioning whether we could open our hands and hearts with faith in the midst of confusion and doubt. To witness to Christ by our lives, we need special help from God. The Sacrament of Confirmation reminds us of that help that comes from God as we witness to God by our lives.

SCRIPTURE REFLECTIONS

Acts 4:5–22   *Without faith in Christ, Peter and John would have trembled before the awesome court of the religious leaders of their day. The leaders realize that they cannot ignore the healing performed by the disciples of Christ, so they attempt to silence them, warning them against preaching about Jesus. Peter and John, however, cannot remain silent. They must follow the higher authority of God and continue their mission to share the message of Christ, even if they must sacrifice their lives for this message.*

What Does This Passage Tell Me about My Life as a Fully Committed Christian?

1 Peter 1:3–12   *Through a gift of God, we share in a new, spiritual birth which fills us with hope. This hope calls us to respond to the gifts of Christ's resurrection as well as the eternal gift of salvation. At times, we will have to suffer pain or ridicule for our faith, but the gifts of sharing in Christ's life which come to us through Christian initiation should lead us to rejoice and not to weep. The prophets prepared the way for our faith in Christ, and now we must prepare the way for those who will come after us.*

How Does This Passage Apply to My Life as a Christian?

70

Mark 8:34–38   *Mark was writing his gospel for Christians undergoing persecution. He reminded them that the true follower of Christ is one who is willing to face all suffering in the same spirit Christ accepted it. We are not called to seek out suffering, but we should be willing to accept sacrifice and suffering in the service of the gospel. Strange as it sounds, the one who lays down his or her life for the sake of the gospel becomes the spiritually successful person. Such a person is a person of service, and the rewards of such dedication touch her or him during this life on earth as well as in heaven.*

What Does the Call to Discipleship Demand in My Daily Life?

MY RESPONSE

The Sacraments of Initiation keep reminding us of our dedication to the mission of Christ. As disciples, we do not face the same situations as Christ, but we face modern situations with the hope of responding to them in the way Christ would respond. As disciples, we are not called to death by crucifixion, we are called to share our lives and the message of Christ with others. As disciples, we are servants in this world as Christ was, and we are called to lay down our lives in many ways for the sake of others. By seeking to serve those in need and accepting the hardships of such service, we are laying down our lives for others.

How Do I Intend to Live as a Disciple in the World?

FURTHER DISCUSSION

1. What meaning does confirmation have in your life today?

2. In what ways should the Church be working for justice in the world?

3. Why is evangelization so important, yet so difficult?

PRAYER

Lord, Strength of Our Life,
you share your message with us
and give us the courage
to share it with others.

Never let us stop sharing your message
through our words
and our lives.

AMEN.

Sacraments of Initiation— Part 3—Eucharist

(In His Light—Chapter Ten)

INTRODUCTION

The third Sacrament of Initiation, the Sacrament of the Eucharist, draws us even more deeply into a life of worship and union with Christ. Baptism and confirmation enable us to worship God by sharing in the priesthood of Christ. Now we come to that worship itself, and through the bread and wine we share in the gift of the sacramental presence of Jesus.

Some people view the sacraments as gifts from God for their own good. But we are reminded that the sacraments are given for the good of others, that we might bring the presence and love of Christ to others. Even the Sacrament of the Eucharist, rather than being seen as a reward for being a good person, should be seen as a help to enable us to live out our commitment as a Christian to love and to assist others.

As is mentioned in the opening reflection to this chapter (*In His Light,* page 143), the Eucharistic celebration is our perfect way of telling God of our love. We need God's help to carry that love into our lives. This comes through sharing in his body and blood.

SCRIPTURE REFLECTIONS

Mark 14:12–26   *Meals had an important role in ancient Jewish practice. To share in a meal with someone was to share his or her life. Mark sets the scene for the Last Supper in the context of the Passover meal. Jesus and his disciples celebrate the feast in unity with all of Judaism. At this meal, Jesus will offer himself as the new lamb of sacrifice. As we celebrate the Eucharist, we place ourselves* in union with Christ and all Christians. To share in this meal with Christ is to share in the life of Christ and to offer our lives as Christ offered his. The meal is a cause for rejoicing, for singing songs, but also a time for commitment to Christ and to those with whom we share the meal.

What Is the Meaning of the Celebration of the Eucharist in My Life?

Acts 2:42–47   The early Church community referred to the Eucharistic meal as the "breaking of the bread." It was not just a moment, but a way of life. In celebrating the meal, they were celebrating the spirit and life of Jesus. This meant that the Eucharist was lived as the community sought to know more about their faith, as they prayed together, as they performed wonders, and as they shared their goods with one another. They saw these activities as a matter of living their faith and commitment expressed through the celebration of the Eucharist.

What Does This Scripture Passage Tell Me about the Role of the Eucharist in My Life?

1 Corinthians 11:17–34   *The selfishness and lack of concern on the part of those gathering for the Eucharist shocks Paul. The very action which should be one of love and concern now stands as their condemnation. Paul sees a contradiction between the action they are celebrating in the Eucharist and their manner of celebrating. The essential love and concern for one another is lacking, and Paul warns them that this makes the Eucharistic celebration a time of condemnation for them, rather than a time of blessing.*

What Does This Passage Tell Me about My Need for Commitment to the Total Idea of Eucharist?

MY RESPONSE

The assembly gathers together to worship God as one. The assembly of God's people is important. We do not join in worship for ourselves alone, but we join as one to pray for all God's people and to glorify God with one unified voice of praise. The Church reminds us of our need to respond as one. Our celebration is not a time for private devotion, but a time for us to join with others in publicly proclaiming praise and thanksgiving to God.

How Do I Intend to Fulfill My Role in the Eucharistic Celebration?

FURTHER DISCUSSION

1. What answer would you give to those who say that Jesus gave us the one perfect sacrifice and that we have no need for a continual celebration of the "sacrifice of the Eucharist"?

2. What answer would you give to those who say that they would rather pray alone during the Eucharistic Celebration and not be bothered with active participation?

3. How do the different seasons of the Church Year affect our attitude toward worship?

PRAYER

Lord, Our Eucharistic Gift,
enable us always to understand your goodness,
to express our love
in, with, and through you
in this gift of the Eucharist.

Guide us
that our Eucharistic Celebration
may always be one of love.

AMEN.

Session Number _____

Date _____

Reconciliation— A New Beginning

(In His Light—Chapter Eleven)

INTRODUCTION

The Sacrament of Reconciliation looks not only at the one who has sinned and is seeking forgiveness, it looks also at the community as the one forgiving. It is a dramatic moment in time, a celebration in which a sinner turns to God and the community to seek forgiveness for sins and to seek God's blessings for a better life in the future. Because we already know of God's love for us, we know that God will forgive us, no matter what we have done in the past. In this act of reconciliation, we not only turn from the past, we also turn to the future, ready to continue living a life in union with Christ through the community.

SCRIPTURE REFLECTIONS

Mark 2:1–12   *To the Jewish people of Jesus' time, ill health was a sign of God's punishment for sin. In the minds of many people, a person with some sickness or physical deformity was surely a sinner. To prove that he could forgive sins, Jesus healed the paralytic. When the crowd saw the healing, they then believed that he had also forgiven the sin. The reaction of the crowd was to praise God for this great wonder.*

What Does This Scripture Passage Tell Me about the Activity of Christ in My Life?

Luke 15:11–32   *Now we look at the one who forgives. The father continuously looked out for the son's return, and when he saw his son in the distance, he ran out to meet him and to embrace him with love. This is God! God looks for the sinner to turn back in repentance and when the sinner returns, God runs off to embrace the sinful person. The elder son does not yet understand the forgiving nature of the father. God would like to have all people understand this love and respond to repentance as God does.*

What Does This Parable Tell Me about My Attitude toward Forgiveness?

John 20:19–23   *Jesus brings "peace" to his disciples. It is not a peace to be kept, but one meant to be shared. The peace offered by Jesus was a deep, abiding peace and one that could remain with his disciples, no matter how much turmoil surrounded them on the outside. The way to this peace was the gift of living in union with Christ. This peace comes with forgiveness of sins. When Jesus offered this peace to his disciples, he also gave them the power to forgive sins.*

How Can a Knowledge That God Forgives My Sins Help Me to Live in Peace in the World, No Matter What Happens?

MY RESPONSE

Loving friendships are important in our lives. When someone expresses love for us, we strive to respond to that love by living up to the expectations of the lover. At times we fail, and we then strive to alleviate the wounds we have inflicted upon the one we love. We attempt to change our way of life so that we will not hurt the loved one again. This is the meaning of reconciliation. It is a means of restoring a friendship wounded by our lack of love.

How Do I Intend to Continue to Reconcile My Life with That of Jesus?

FURTHER DISCUSSION

1. What answer would you give to those who feel that it is not necessary to seek the ministry of the ordained priest in reconciling our lives with that of Christ and the Church?

2. What is your reaction to the idea that the Sacrament of Reconciliation is a celebration?

3. What are some examples of acts of reconciliation which take place between friends?

PRAYER

Lord, Our Forgiving Companion,
you live with us in our life
even when we turn our hearts
against you.
Teach us to understand the celebration
of returning to you
and living our lives
in your love.
AMEN.

Marriage and the Family
(In His Light—Chapter Twelve)

INTRODUCTION

A social worker told an audience that he had at one time experienced the sorrow of so many painful, separated families in his work that he had become bitter about marriage. In fact, he actually reached a stage where he would rather attend a funeral than a marriage. At a funeral, all pain was ended; at a marriage, he felt it was just beginning. In time, however, he came upon some successful marriages and even some successful victims of separated families, and he realized how the family had some rewards to offer. The different ingredient in the happy marriage, he reported to the audience, was not the lack of disillusionment or pain, but the ability to confront the difficulty and call in help when needed. The successful victims of a separated family, whether they were the spouses or the children, could also point to someone who guided them through the moment of difficulty. It was not pain that was to be avoided in life, but the successful response to that pain that was needed. He smiled and told the audience that his faith in marriage was renewed—so much so, that he married and now has three children.

In the opening story to this chapter (*In His Light*, page 177), we read of a marriage that lasted fifty years. Despite the pain, frustration, anger, boredom, and doubt, this couple found in life the great meaning and the great reward of true love. Others helped this couple reach this point of celebration in their lives, but they themselves could point to God as their main support.

SCRIPTURE REFLECTIONS

Song of Songs 2:1–17 *Although this book is actually speaking of God's love for the chosen people, it speaks in most intimate detail about a human, romantic love found* among new lovers. For some, the book is an embarrassment in its open expressions of romantic love, yet it is presented as a type of love worthy of God. In these verses, the loved one knows how important she is to her lover, and yet she must await the lover rather than force him to act. When the lover comes, he bounds across the hills, showing how anxious he is to be with his beloved. We are the loved ones, and God is the lover.

What Does This Passage Tell Me about the Value of My Experiences of Loving and Being Loved?

Luke 2:41–52   Although we know very little about the home life of Jesus, we do know that Mary and Joseph nurtured him as a good Jew. In this passage, Luke tells us that they took him to Jerusalem each year for the feast of the Passover. The message of this narrative is far more important than the events used to describe it. Although Mary had raised Jesus and knew him well, she continued to encounter his unexplained ways of acting. Luke is telling us that Jesus experienced his vocation early in life. Like many mothers of her own day and our day, Mary had to reflect upon these confusing new directions which arose in her son's life.

What Message for Parents Can We Learn from This Passage?

Ephesians 5:25–33   *In this passage, Paul has a new message for Christian husbands. They should not act like masters over their wives, but should love them as they love their own bodies. Even more, they should love their wives as Christ loved the Church, the people of God on earth. Because of this love, God made marriage and family life central to the plan of creation. The two become one, they love each other as they love themselves, and through this love they become an image of Christ's love for the world. What more could be said of marriage?*

What Does This Passage Tell Me about the Sacrament of Marriage?

MY RESPONSE

Someone once said that we can measure the health of a nation by measuring the success of its family life. In our country today, we have many different types of families. Some families are two-parent families, while others are single-parent families. In some cases, a man or woman must care for the family alone because a spouse has divorced or passed away. Whatever the situation, marriage as a sacrament calls all people to live their dedication to family as perfectly as the situation allows. Everyone in the family, married as well as unmarried, child as well as parent, plays an important role. Our family has shaped us, and we shape others by our way of acting in the family. Family life is not a simple dedication which we can take lightly. It is central to God's creation.

How Do I Intend to Fulfill My Role in the Family?

FURTHER DISCUSSION

1. Why is it important to know the purpose of marriage?

2. Why is it sometimes necessary to emphasize that sexuality is God's idea and not the devil's idea?

3. What do you feel are some fallacies and some truths about family planning?

PRAYER

Lord, God of Love,
you share your life with us
and teach us the meaning of love.
Guide families
that they may learn from you
the demands
as well as the rewards
of love.
AMEN.

A Ministry of Service
(In His Light—Chapter Thirteen)

INTRODUCTION

One of the greatest compliments paid to missionaries in foreign countries comes when people refer to them as "one of our own." Not every missionary receives this great honor, but some are able to enter so fully into the daily joys and tragedies of the people they serve that they receive this gifted title. Father Damian who lived among the lepers and eventually became a leper himself is a good example of a missionary whom the people could easily refer to as "one of our own."

As we look to Christ, we discover a true missionary. Jesus became "one of our own" as he came to share our human life with all its joys and sufferings. All Christians, as followers of Christ, are called to enter fully into the human experience, to rejoice and suffer with the joys and tragedies of other members of the human family. Through our baptism, we are called not only to proclaim Christ, but to live as Christ lived—as a totally dedicated missionary in the service of the world.

SCRIPTURE REFLECTIONS

1 Corinthians 12:4–11   *When a child is learning to swim, parents or teachers must be nearby to assure the child that they will save him or her if anything happens. When we accept the call to service, and ministry, we too need assurance that someone will be there to save us if anything goes wrong. God not only saves us, but gives us the gifts of the Holy Spirit. Through these gifts we grow more like Christ. Just as the Spirit led Christ victoriously through his trials, so* the Spirit leads us through our lives as servants for the sake of others.

What Does This Scripture Passage Say Concerning Your Life and Your Call to Service?

John 13:1–17   The story of the Last Supper found in John's Gospel tells us nothing about the meal itself, although it tells us about the spirit of the Eucharist which is also a spirit of service. Jesus washes the feet of his disciples and tells them that they must do the same. It is not just washing feet, but it is a call to minister and serve in all areas of life in the name of Christ. This passage links Eucharist with ministry.

In What Ways Can I Follow Jesus' Example in Serving Others?

Matthew 9:35–38 *God fills the world with gifts, but Jesus reminds us that God needs dedicated men and women to nourish and gather these gifts. This passage is a reminder for all of us to pray continuously that the Lord will send into the world people totally dedicated to the harvest that they might gather the ignorant, the weak, the poor, and the spiritually and physically sick into God's reign. Our need for totally dedicated laity, men religious, women religious, and presbyters is great. It will demand sacrifice, and our prayers will support them in this sacrifice.*

What Does This Scripture Passage Ask of My Life?

MY RESPONSE

The tendency for many is to leave the ministry to the presbyters (ordained priests), and women religious (sisters) and men religious (brothers). The Church today, however, is making us all more aware of our call to ministry. Instead of waiting to be called, we can search out ways of helping and we can volunteer our services to ministry. We can also serve by fulfilling our particular roles in life in a more perfect manner for the sake of Christ.

How Do I Intend to Live As a Member of a Ministering Community, Dedicated to the Mission of Christ?

FURTHER DISCUSSION

1. Do you see any difference between the ordained ministry and the ministry of all the faithful which comes to us through our baptism?

2. What are some possible ministries in which you could share?

3. How do you feel the Pope, bishops, ordained priests, and deacons should perform their ministerial roles in the world today?

PRAYER

Lord, Giver of Gifts,
you shared your life with us
as a servant
and you suffered for us.
Grant us the faith,
the courage
and the love
to accept your life
in our life
that we may serve you
and others
as you have served us.
AMEN.

Anointing of the Sick

(In His Light—Chapter Fourteen)

INTRODUCTION

A visitor to a religious healing service wrote an article on her experience for a leading religious magazine. She told how she had gone to the service with no ailment of her own except a great skepticism concerning the proclaimed healings which were taking place at these ceremonies. The service lasted several hours during which time people prayed together and sang hymns. Throughout the service, the healings took place, some visibly, some within the person. But the visitor spoke of a chilling sensation. Without investigating the truth of the healings, which was the reason for her coming, she began to feel peace and no longer cared whether or not she could prove the truth. She had experienced God. She had changed. She had been healed. She left that service with a new view about life and about God.

We often read of other types of healings which are just as important as the healing mentioned above. The kind touch of a relative, a friend, or a concerned person brings healing. Healing comes through the hands of the doctor, the nurse, or a hospital visitor. In God's creation, we have many different experiences of God's healing touch.

SCRIPTURE REFLECTIONS

Matthew 8:14—17   *Jesus healed Peter's mother-in-law of an apparently simple fever. She not only accepted his healing, but responded to it. She got up at once and waited on Jesus. Jesus continues to heal. He took upon himself the sickness and sufferings of all people as the prophet had foretold. Whatever role we play in sharing the healing of God* with others, we must follow the example of Christ's compassion to be true healers.

What Message for My Life Can I Learn from This Story of the Healing of Peter's Mother-in-law?

Acts 3:1–10   Peter had no coin to give to the cripple, but he had much more. He had the gift of healing. We ourselves might not have the gift of helping a physical cripple, but we can help the spiritually crippled. With Peter, we reach out to offer what we have. Through our prayers, our kindness, and our compassion, we can also say to the spiritually crippled, "In the name of Jesus Christ the Nazarene, walk."

How Does My Faith in Jesus Bring Healing to Others?

James 5:13–20   *James encourages the suffering person to pray and the sick person to seek anointing and prayers from the presbyters. The Church sees in this the scriptural reference to the Sacrament of the Anointing of the Sick. It brings healing and forgiveness of sins. Everyone should have confidence in the healing power of prayer and should seek to bring the sinner to spiritual healing. A true healing is not just a healing of the body, but also a healing of the spirit.*

How Does the Understanding of the Community Aspect of the Anointing of the Sick Affect My Thoughts about This Sacrament?

MY RESPONSE

Concern for the sick and suffering, whether in body or spirit, is central to the Church. Through Christ, the Church brings comfort and healing to those in need, and we all take part in this healing through our prayers as a community. The Church can reach out to the sick and suffering through its presbyters, its visitors to the sick, and its praying community. Whenever any member of the community acts with concern for the sick, the whole community acts.

How Do I Intend to Show Concern for the Sick and Suffering through My Role in the Community?

FURTHER DISCUSSION

1. At what point would you call on a presbyter (an ordained priest) to anoint a sick relative or friend, and what would be your role in the anointing ceremony?

2. Why is it important for the faithful to understand the meaning of Holy Viaticum?

3. What are your thoughts about the idea of communal anointing of the sick?

PRAYER

Lord, God of Compassion,
you share with us
your healing power
to heal our bodies
and our spirits.
Continually give us healing
against the allurements of the world
that we may know your goodness,
compassion
and love.
AMEN.

Death to Life
(In His Light — Chapter Fifteen)

INTRODUCTION

Besides the study about those who are nearing the moment of death, another study of experiences from people who have apparently died, but have been revived, has left us with some startling considerations. Many people tell of hovering over their own body while the doctors and nurses worked to bring them back to life. Others tell of coming down a dark tunnel to a peaceful light in which they meet some friends or relatives who have preceded them in death. Those who have this "near-death" experience live the rest of their lives no longer afraid of death.

Death will visit all of us at some unknown moment in our lives. Our faith or lack of faith will deeply affect the manner in which we meet our death. Because we know that we must face death, we pay more attention to these near-death experiences with hope of gaining some insight into death. The person of faith, however, is able to find some answers and an abiding hope in the Scriptures.

SCRIPTURE REFLECTIONS

1 Thessalonians 4:13–17   *When the people of Thessalonica fear that those who have already died will miss the Second Coming of Christ, Paul assures them that the dead will be raised on the last day. Those who experience death before the Second Coming will be raised along with those who are still alive, and all will share in God's glory. It is this message of resurrection which inspires Paul to comfort the fears of the people.*

What Does This Passage Tell Me about the Fears or Joys I Experience When Thinking of the Second Coming of Christ?

Revelation 21:1–8   In the language of apocalyptic writings, the author speaks of a new heaven and a new earth at the end of time. It will be a land without end and a land without the sufferings of this world. Christ will be there to refresh those who call on him. This victory of gaining heaven will exist for all those who remained faithful to God. For those who did not remain faithful, there will be a second death, that is, an eternal death in the fiery pool of burning sulphur. We should not take this apocalyptic language literally, but we should heed its message—an eternal reward and joy for the faithful and an eternal anguish and pain for those who are unfaithful.

What Does This Passage Tell Me about the Joys of the Resurrection?

John 14:1—7 *Jesus refers to heaven as his "Father's house" and tells his disciples that there are many dwellings there. This tells that there are many different people who will be dwelling in God's eternal home. The path to this dwelling is the life and person of Jesus himself.*

How Can I Apply the Message of This Passage to My Life?

MY RESPONSE

Death is a fact of life which gives a sense of urgency to our lives. We have a mission to perform, and God offers us time and special gifts to fulfill this mission. Without death, we would never have any "deadlines" to meet, and we could put off the use of our gifts as long as we wanted. Death, however, is our path to resurrection and glory in Christ. We do not live to die, but we live to build up this world and share Christ's message until the day we enter eternal glory. We have a mission to perform, and we have hope given to us by Jesus that an unimaginable life of joy and love will be ours for all eternity.

How Do I Intend to Make the Thought of Death a Positive Influence in My Life?

FURTHER DISCUSSION

1. How would you describe your image of heaven and hell?

2. What are your thoughts about the idea of purgatory?

3. How do you feel about the Second Coming of Christ?

PRAYER

Lord God, Our Heavenly Dwelling,
fill us with a love
and a desire
to be with you
for all eternity,
but let this love
inspire us to work that others
may share this joy with us.
AMEN.

Session Number _____

Date _____

First Sunday of Lent

INTRODUCTION

Fred is an alcoholic. One night, at an Alcoholics Anonymous meeting, Fred told of the destruction wrought by alcohol in his life. His wife had divorced him, his grown children disowned him, his friends abandoned him, and his boss fired him. One friend, however, persuaded Fred to seek help in a resort for alcoholics, and after two months Fred returned home, sober and anxious to share his experiences in an effort to help others live a normal life, despite the disease of alcoholism. In his comments at the Alcoholics Anonymous meeting, Fred told the group, "I went off into the desert and faced all the devils inside myself. I won and now I'm a new man ready to live life."

The readings for this First Sunday of Lent invite us to move immediately into the desert and to face the devil within us. They challenge us to face the power of evil in the world with the power and example of Jesus Christ.

SCRIPTURE REFLECTIONS

Year A

Matthew 4:1–11   *In the Old Testament, the Israelites in the desert failed to overcome temptation to sin. In the New Testament, Jesus reverses the situation as he overcomes the temptations of the evil one in the desert. In this story, the devil is attempting to lure Jesus into abandoning his mission, which is to confront the power of evil in the world. The message reminds us that temptation to evil not only seeks to lead us into sin, but it attempts to lead us away from our mission in life.*

What Does This Scripture Passage Tell Me about Temptation in My Life?

Genesis 2:7–9, 3:1–7   The story found in the opening chapters of the Book of Genesis tells us the message of God's creation of human beings and the arrival of sin in the world. Human beings were created to the image and likeness of God, that is, they had the ability to think, judge, act, and choose freely and independently of others. These human beings, however, brought sin into the world by seeking to be even more like God. As a result of the first sin in the world, evil gained a grip, and human beings hid themselves from God and from each other. It was this power of evil that Jesus confronted in the desert.

How Might I Be Responsible for Allowing Sin to Gain Control in My World?

Romans 5:12–19   *Once a person sinned, evil (spiritual death) entered the world and gained a more secure grip as others began to sin. Although the law of Moses did not exist from the beginning, Paul is telling his listeners that there was a law written in the hearts of all people, allowing them to know what was sinful. The gift of new life which came from the person of Christ, however, far outdistanced any of the evil effects of sin in the world. As Christians, we place our hope in this gift which comes from Christ. In our confrontation with evil, we join with Christ in bringing a new and more wonderful gift to the world.*

How May I Use the Gift of Christ's Blessings in Overcoming Sin in the World?

Year B

Mark 1:12–15   *Mark offers a brief description of Jesus' encounter with Satan in the desert. Jesus would live in a world filled with evil and danger (beasts), but he overcame the power of evil because God was with him (angels). In overcoming the temptation, Jesus remained faithful to sharing his message that the "reign of God is at hand." This episode reminds us of our call to overcome evil, not only for the sake of winning over evil, but for the sake of the mission to which Jesus calls us.*

How Do I Serve Others When I Avoid Sin?

Genesis 9:8–15   *God never allows sin to conquer completely. In the midst of the growing power of sin as recorded in the first eleven chapters of the Book of Genesis, God offers a rainbow, a ray of hope in the form of a covenant. Through this covenant, God promises to protect the people of the earth from the powers of evil. The covenant will last as long as there are rainbows.*

What Hope Can I Gain from This Scripture Passage?

1 Peter 3:18–22   *The covenant God made with the people of ancient times reaches its fulfillment in Christ. Christ died to bring life; he went down into the abyss and was raised to new life which he shares with us through baptism. Just as the waters of the flood symbolized God's love and salvation of all people, so baptism in Christ brings salvation to us. Like Noah, we come to a new beginning, but ours is a spiritual rebirth, not a physical one.*

How Is My Passing Through the Waters of Baptism to My Ministry Similar to Christ's Passage through the Desert to His Ministry?

100

Luke 4:1–13   *Under the guidance of the Holy Spirit, Jesus overcomes the temptations of the devil in the desert. The devil tempts him to come to power by feeding the hungry (turning stone to bread), by using the power of the world (paying homage to Satan), or by forcing God's hand so that God must act in a miraculous way (throwing himself from the parapet of the temple). Jesus remains obedient to his mission, refusing to accept worldly power and seeking only the will of God.*

How Does This Passage Apply to My Struggle to Follow the Will of God in My Life?

Deuteronomy 26:4–10   *Moses urges the people to honor God for all the gifts God has bestowed on the nation. He calls them to a memorial of past events, when God overcame the great power of Egypt and led the people to salvation through the desert. Because they have received so much from God, Moses calls them to return some of these gifts to God in order to show their gratitude and trust.*

What Attitude toward the Goods of This World Can I Gain from This Passage?

Romans 10:8–13   *Once we recognize that our greatest gifts rest in serving God rather than in serving our own desire for power, we will share fully in salvation given us by Christ. Salvation speaks not only of life hereafter, but also of this life. If our lives and our words faithfully proclaim the presence of Christ in the world, we are living the salvation given us by Christ.*

What Do I Consider to Be the Real Gifts in My Life?

MY RESPONSE

Our life is a form of desert, a time when we struggle with temptation, yet experience comfort and strength in the midst of temptation. We trust that God is with us, guiding us to place our treasure in the gifts of God rather than in the power of the world. We share in Jesus' call to restore the true image and likeness of God to human creation. We do this by following the message and example of Jesus Christ.

How Do I Intend to Make This Journey through Lent a Time for Following in the Footsteps of Christ?

FURTHER DISCUSSION

1. In what way is the desert a good example of life?

2. If you had to develop the theme of the readings for the First Sunday of Lent in order to preach to others, what story or examples would you use to clarify the theme?

3. What are some examples of the power of sin in the world?

PRAYER

Lord, Giver of New Life,
you overcame the temptations of an evil world
to show the world the goodness
of your creation.

Give us the strength,
the courage,
and the insight
to follow your example
in overcoming evil
and bringing new life
into the world . . .

AMEN.

Second Sunday of Lent

INTRODUCTION

When we meet someone, we form immediate impressions. As we get to know the person more intimately, those impressions often change and we come to a newer and deeper knowledge of the individual. We often discover a more compassionate, a more loving, and a more understanding person than we ever imagined.

As we live our life with Christ, we come to know a more compassionate, a more loving, and a more understanding Person. In many ways, Christ becomes much more than we first imagined. The reason is that we ourselves are always changing and we are coming to know Christ in a more intimate way. Under the guidance of the Spirit, Christ is becoming more important to our lives.

On this Sunday, we celebrate the theme of the Transfiguration of Jesus. The disciples saw Jesus in a different light. They knew Jesus as their human companion and leader who journeyed with them, but now, through faith, they knew him as the glorified Christ who is also God.

As Christians, we continually strive to understand Christ in all his grandeur without losing sight of the fact that he humbled himself and came among us as a servant.

SCRIPTURE REFLECTIONS

Year A

Matthew 17:1–9 *The story of the Transfiguration of Jesus is a post-resurrection story. It portrays Jesus as he was understood by the early Church after his resurrection. The disciples had followed Jesus, lived with Jesus and listened to Jesus. Now they caught a glimpse of the glory of Jesus, and they understood so much more.*

105

In this vision, they are directed to listen to Jesus, to hear what he has to say, and to act upon what is heard. We too must travel to the mountain with Jesus. We must look into his mystery, strive to understand its meaning and seek to bring that vision of Jesus into the mainstream of our life. "Lord, it is good for us to be here!"

How Can I Become More Conscious of the Presence of Christ in the World Today?

Genesis 12:1—4   At the age of seventy-five, Abram changed his life and set out at the call of God to a new life of faith. Abram is considered the father of the people of God in the Old Testament and the great ancestor of Christianity in the New Testament. Because of his new life of faith, God promises Abram that he will be the father of a great nation. God calls to Abram who responds in faith to God and changes his life for God.

How Does the Story of Abram's Faith Help Me to Gain a More Honest View of God's Creation?

2 Timothy 1:8—10   Paul writes this letter to Timothy from prison, reminding Timothy that God has called them to a new life simply because God wanted it and not because of any meritorious act on their part. Now, through the light of the Gospel, the true call of the world to salvation and holiness can be seen. For those of us who can see this presence of God in the world and keep firm in the faith, it is a type of "transfiguration" of the world. "Lord, it is good for us to be here!"

What Does This Scripture Passage Tell Me about the Gift of Faith Which Enables Me to See Christ's Presence in My Life?

Year B

Mark 9:2—10   In this story of the Transfiguration, we catch a glimpse of the glory of Christ. When the disciples see Jesus in his glory along with Elijah and Moses, they also hear a voice which bids them to listen to Christ, the beloved Son of God. Once we understand the true person of Jesus by looking beyond his humanness to his divinity, we realize that he truly speaks the words of life to us. This transfiguration allows us to live with faith and to see the true meaning of life.

How Can I Apply the Message of the Transfiguration to My Life?

Genesis 22:1–2, 9–13, 15–18   *When God asked Abraham to sacrifice his son, the man of faith must have felt deep pain and confusion. He would not only sacrifice a beloved son, he would also be ending any claim to having true offspring. Abraham knew that God had promised that his offspring would be as numerous as the stars, yet God was now asking him to destroy the only one who would make this possible. Despite his confusion, Abraham was prepared to act with faith, trusting that God would provide an answer.*

How Does My Faith Compare with That of Abraham?

Romans 8:31–34   *In the story of Abraham and Isaac, God held back Abraham's hand and saved Isaac. Jesus, through his death, gains numerous spiritual offspring for God, and he sits enthroned in a position of glory. His position of glory, however, is not for him alone, but for us. Jesus continually intercedes for us before God.*

How Does Faith in Christ Fill Me with Hope?

Year C

Luke 9:28–36   When the disciples experience the *transfiguration of Jesus, they are so overcome with awe that they are ready to remain in this glory with Jesus. In the course of the experience, they hear the voice of God stating, "This is my Son, my Chosen One." The author of this Gospel concerns himself with the idea of being chosen. Jesus, chosen by God, fulfills his mission perfectly. Now, with the insight of faith, we are the chosen ones called to fulfill the mission of Christ on earth.*

How Does the Message of the Transfiguration Help Me to Live My Life in Faith?

Genesis 15:5–12, 17–18   *When God tells Abraham that his offspring will be as numerous as the stars, Abraham immediately trusts God. Because of this faith, God enters a covenant with Abraham by which they bind themselves to each other. In order to have a covenant, we must first have faith.*

What Does This Need for Faith Tell Me about My Covenants in Life?

Philippians 3:17—4:1   *Paul laments the fact that some have chosen the way of the world over the way of God. Others, however, live in the spirit of heaven, longing for the coming of Christ who will bring them to glory. These are those who live with faith.*

How Does My Faith Influence My Attitude toward Life?

MY RESPONSE

Living with faith means seeing the world as it truly is, a world created by God and a world filled with the spirit of Christ. We cannot see this with our eyes, but we can "transfigure" the world with the eyes of faith. When we live by faith, we can come closer to the true meaning of life and the gifts of life. With faith, we are able to fulfill our mission in life, trusting that God is with us.

How Do I Intend to Open My Life to Christ through Faith?

FURTHER DISCUSSION

1. What are some of the messages you find in the story of the Transfiguration?

2. If you were to preach a homily on the idea of faith, what stories or examples would you use to develop the theme?

3. Would you say that faith is dominant in our world today?

PRAYER

Lord, God of Inner Light,
you stand transfigured before your disciples,
displaying yourself in all your glory.
Help us to see you transfigured
in the world
before us.

Help us to discover you
in those surprising moments of *our* life,
when you suddenly allow us to see
YOU
in our world,
and understand your presence
in our lives.
AMEN.

Third Sunday of Lent

INTRODUCTION

Now that we have entered the desert under the direction of the Spirit, and have looked at Christ's presence in the world around us, we look to Jesus as a source of life to help us live our lives as dedicated Christians. We can become so logical about our lives, how we should plan, how we should save, how we should appear, and so forth. But there is a logic the Christian follows that simply asks, "How should we serve God?" To seek to satisfy ourselves with material goods always leaves us thirsting for more. To satisfy our lives with Christ leaves us fulfilled, striving continually to grow, but content in the gifts God has given us.

SCRIPTURE REFLECTIONS

Year A

John 4:5–42   *As Jesus rests by the well, he offers the Samaritan woman the living waters. The living waters come from Christ, and they symbolize for the writer of the Gospel the waters of baptism. The gift of Christ is not limited to Jews nor to men alone, but to all people. In a manner of a true conversion, the woman accepts Jesus' word and brings others to listen to Christ. These others came to faith in Jesus because of the message he preached, rather than because of his ability to tell the woman all about her life.*

In What Way Does Baptism Become the "Living Waters" for Me?

Exodus 17:3–7   When Moses strikes the rock, the life-giving waters flow forth for the people in the desert. God provides for the people in the desert, but at times they try to force God's hand. They lack faith, and they complain against Moses. The tone of the passage reminds us of God's anger with the people.

What Lesson for My Life Can I Learn from This Passage?

Romans 5:1–2, 5–8   *Because of his love for us, Jesus died and was raised to bring us these life-giving waters. Through baptism, we can boast of God's love for us. We do not boast of our own accomplishments, but we can boast of Christ acting in, with, and through us in the power of the Holy Spirit. Because Christ died for us when we were sinful and powerless, we have a right to boast about Christ.*

In What Way Can I Boast about Christ in My Life?

Year B

John 2:13–25   *The act of cleansing the temple of the money changers is seen as a "sign" by the people. Although the event was not miraculous, it showed the power of Jesus. It was because of his concern for the house of God and the authority of his words that the people placed their faith in Jesus.*

What Led Me to Place My Faith in Jesus?

Exodus 20:1–17   *Conversion demands more than words; it demands deeds. When the people of Israel escaped from the slavery of Egypt, they were taking a risk in trusting God. As a nation, they not only proclaimed God, but they showed their trust by setting down norms or deeds which would identify them as a people of God. The commandments given to Moses in the desert established the norms for ways of acting in the desert and in Palestine. Their conversion was not only one of words, but it was one of deeds, one that deeply affected their way of life as a community.*

What Are Some Signs of My Continual Conversion to Christ?

1 Corinthians 1:22–25   *The "signs" and "wisdom" of Christianity are hardly those of the world. Christians preach a message of a founder who failed by allowing the powers of the world to overcome him. People of faith, however, recognize the power of the resurrection and the triumph of the resurrection. Christians call others to conversion to the cross, the need to be willing to suffer as Christ suffered for the sake of the reign of God. This is foolishness, but it is the true meaning of conversion.*

How Does Conversion to a Crucified Christ Affect My Life?

Year C

Luke 13:1–9   *God is not anxious to condemn us. When we commit ourselves to Christ, God has certain expectations of us. We are meant to bear good fruit in the world through our good deeds and our love for one another. If we do not bear good fruit in the world, God is willing to give us more time with hope so that we can be faithful to our call. After a period of time, however, if we do not bear that good fruit, we shall be cut down.*

How Can I Fulfill My Call in Bearing Good Fruit in the World?

Exodus 3:1–8   *God called the people of Israel to commitment to the covenant through Moses. God told Moses that he should lead the people of Israel out of slavery, and that they should know that they are God's chosen people. He is the God of Abraham, Isaac, and Jacob, the God who continues to care for the Israelite nation. This narrative tells us of God's faithfulness to the covenant made with Abraham, Isaac, and Jacob. God is a faithful God.*

What Hope for My Life Can I Gain from This Passage?

1 Corinthians 10:1–6, 10–12 *Not all who commit themselves to conversion remain faithful to God. This passage gives us a warning that words alone are not enough; we must perform the deeds of a Christian. The people of Israel were the chosen people, yet many were lost because they did not live up to their commitment. Paul warns us that we too could sin in the same way.*

How Does This Passage Help Me to Know More about My Commitment as a Christian?

MY RESPONSE

The call of Christ comes as a gift, but it also makes demands on us. As we commit ourselves to Christ, we also realize that God has the right to ask us to live up to that commitment. As Christians, we are expected to reflect the life and message of Jesus in our lives.

How Do I Intend to Live Up to My Commitment as a Christian?

FURTHER DISCUSSION

1. What role does baptism play in your commitment to God?

2. If you were to develop a homily on the theme of conversion and commitment, what stories or examples from life would you use to develop your theme?

3. How do you imagine God acting when people do not live up to their commitments?

PRAYER

Lord, Source of All Life,

guide us in our life
that we might always be mindful of you
in our ministry,
in our prayer,
and in our moments of rest,
knowing that you minister with us,
pray with us,
and rest with us.
AMEN.

Fourth Sunday of Lent

INTRODUCTION

The weeks of Lent are building closer to Easter. This week, we challenge the depth of faith in our lives. Although we know that God is continuously present in the world, we must admit that there are times when we forget about God, times when success or personal gain forge their grip on our lives. For a time, we live in darkness until we again open our eyes to God's light and love.

But the challenge to faith goes even deeper. For the one who truly believes, life becomes restless. We feel the need to share the great gift we have received. The true believer does not just proclaim faith in Jesus Christ and then sit back to celebrate the soft-chair comfort of this gift. The gift of faith must be lived and shared.

SCRIPTURE REFLECTIONS

Year A

John 9:1–41 *Jesus not only cures the blind man, but he sends him to the pool "Siloam" which means "one who has been sent." The blind man becomes the model for all who receive the gift of faith. They are sent! The Pharisees represent those who are still in darkness and have no faith in Jesus. They cling to the world and cause pain and confusion for people of faith. The full meaning behind the healing of the blind man becomes evident when he is able to proclaim his spiritual sight that leads him to profess his faith in Jesus. Once we have faith, we too are sent!*

As One Who Is Sent, How Well Do I Share My Faith with Others?

1 Samuel 16:1, 6–7, 10–13 *To live by faith means to live with a spiritual insight into the world. Samuel is warned not to make his judgment on appearances alone, but to judge with the insight of God. When appearances become important to us in our lives, we lose a great gift, namely the spiritual insight which enables us to understand the world through God's eyes. Samuel chooses a great king for Israel because of faith, his spiritual insight.*

How Well Am I Able to Judge by God's Standards and not by the Standards of the World?

Ephesians 5:8–14   *At one time, the people of the world lived in darkness, that is, under the power of evil. Now, light has come into the world through Jesus Christ. The true Christian should want to walk by this light, avoiding the dark shadows of worldly enticements. We want to live with Christ. Like a person who was once asleep to God, the Christian now awakes to the joy of the light and follows Christ, the Light of the World.*

How Do I Help Others Live by the Light of Faith?

Year B

John 3:14–21   *The death of Jesus should lead us to faith in the love of Christ. We should see Jesus not as one who comes to condemn us, but as one who willingly lays down his life to show his love for us. If we reject the love of God, then we have condemned ourselves. If we accept Christ and live by the light of faith in Christ, we will live as true disciples of Christ.*

As I Practice My Faith, Why Is It Important for Me to Remember All That Christ Did?

2 Chronicles 36:14–17, 19–23   *This passage is a summary of the destruction of Judea and the call for the Israelites to return home. Because of the lack of faith on the part of their leaders, all of Israel came under the control of foreign powers. The author sees Cyrus, the king of Persia, acting under the inspiration of God when he gives the people a chance to rebuild their lost temple and city. It is an opportunity to build their faith anew, and it is offered to those willing to take advantage of this opportunity.*

What Does This Passage Tell Me about My Struggles in Being Faithful to God?

Ephesians 2:4–10   *The gifts we have received have come from the goodness of God, not through any merit of our own. Our response is to recognize these gifts and to have faith that they are present in our lives. Only in faith will we properly use the gifts God has given us. The gift of living in Christ is the greatest gift, and it is this gift which we must share with others.*

Why Is It Important for Me to Believe That God Has Truly Joined My Life to That of Christ?

Year C

Luke 15:1–3, 11–32   As a loving parent, the father not only forgives the prodigal son, but he fully accepts him back into the family. The elder son, although he dutifully performs his tasks, is not yet prepared to take possession of the inheritance since he lacks the forgiving spirit of the family, as shown by the father. Our call is not simply to follow the rules, but to live in the spirit of the loving parent in this story.

How Can I Capture the Spirit of the Loving Parent in My Life?

Joshua 5:9–12   When the people of Israel celebrated their first passover in the promised land by eating the produce of the land, the manna ceased. The passage reminds us that God helps us in this world until we are able to care for ourselves. When God determines that the family of God is now ready to help themselves while recognizing God's help in their lives, the miracles cease and a new type of miracle takes place—the miracle of people working together in the loving spirit of God.

What Does This Scripture Passage Tell Me about Trusting God in My Daily Life?

2 Corinthians 5:17—21 *Although the world lived in sin, God still reached out in forgiveness to the world. Through an act of reconciliation, God called us to share in a new life of baptism. As a result of this call, we reconcile our lives to God and respond to the gift of new life which is baptism. God calls us not only to avoid sin, God also calls us to a new relationship through Jesus Christ.*

How Can My Life Reflect the Spirit of Christ in All That I Do?

MY RESPONSE

"Living by faith" does not simply mean that we believe in God; it also means that our lives faithfully reflect the spirit of Christ. We bring the world to Christ, not only by proclaiming that we know that Christ is God and that he suffered, died, and was raised, but also by living as a faithful member of Christ's family, reflecting the spirit of God.

How Do I Intend to Live in the Spirit of Christ?

FURTHER DISCUSSION

1. What do you think is demanded of a person who claims to live by faith?

2. If you were to develop a homily on the theme of Christian living, what stories or examples from life would you use to develop your theme?

3. Why is faith necessary for your spiritual growth?

PRAYER

Lord, Light of Our Life,
you call yourself the light in darkness
and you have brought a new light of love
into our world . . .
Teach us to share that light with others,
that they might find in us
the light of encouragement
and support
needed to live in your light.
AMEN.

128

Fifth Sunday of Lent

INTRODUCTION

When a man began his hunger strike for the right of his fellow prisoners to justice and humane treatment, no one paid attention. When the days became weeks and the weeks became months and the hunger strike continued, people became concerned. People who never knew of this man forty days earlier now begged the country leaders to do something about his slow death and about the situation for which he was starving himself. When the officials did change some prison rules for the better, it was too late and the man died. In a sense, however, his death was not in vain. Because of it, others were able to live in a more humane way.

As we draw near to the passion of Jesus, the liturgy becomes more intense in its readings. It speaks about death and life, and reminds us that Jesus, through his death and resurrection, came to give us life.

SCRIPTURE REFLECTIONS

Year A

John 11:1–45   *That Lazarus has already been in the tomb four days attests to the fact that he has really died. The miracle points to an even greater event that will take place in the person of Jesus himself, namely his own resurrection from the dead. There are so many types of death we all face in our lives, deaths that come in the form of loss of jobs, broken family ties, lowered financial status, poor health, or the death of a person we love and even need. For the Christian, such moments cause grief and difficulty, but they also remind us that Jesus is our "resurrection and life." With the raising of Lazarus, we* are reminded that this resurrection is not just a spiritual one, but also a human event which enables us to face and overcome seemingly impossible situations. With Martha, we must proclaim our faith that Jesus is the "Messiah, the Son of God" who has come into the world to give us hope.

What Hope Can I Find in the Story of Jesus' Raising Lazarus from the Dead?

Ezekiel 37:12–14   Ezekiel has just finished his prophecy concerning the dry bones of Israel which God will bring back to life. The Israelites are at their lowest point, living in exile with their hope in God slowly ebbing away. But God is going to bring them to a new life. He is going to do the impossible, bring about a physical resurrection of a nation. They will return from the graves of their exile to the land of Israel and new life. This will be one of the many deaths and resurrections that Israel must face as it plods toward the coming of the Messiah.

What Hope Can I Find for the Community in This Passage from Ezekiel?

Romans 8:8–11   In this letter, "living in the flesh" means living with one's whole life immersed in sin and the lure of the world. But the Christian is living in the Spirit, concerned with the ways of God and believing in God's presence in this world. If we live with the Spirit of Christ throughout our lives, then this same Spirit will bring us to eternal life.

How Does "Living in the Spirit" Affect My Life?

Year B

John 12:20–33   Some Greeks ask to see Jesus. Thus, Jesus shares a message with all of us, allowing us to see him as he truly is. Jesus states that his true identity is that of one who offers his life for the sake of bearing fruit for those whom he loves. He is like the grain of wheat which must die to bear much fruit. It is because of this offering of Jesus that God will glorify Jesus, and in this glorification, we will all see him as he truly is, the Son of God who brought redemption through his life, death, and resurrection.

If Someone Wished to Know Me in Relation to My Special Call in Life, What Would I Tell Them?

Jeremiah 31:31–34   *The day will come when God will make a new covenant with the chosen people. The covenant will not come in the form of written tablets, but in the form of a new way of life written in the hearts of all followers. People will recognize God's chosen ones by the way they act and not by the laws they have written down. In this covenant, their love of God will be their real identity.*

Is My Covenant with God One That Affects the Daily Actions of My Life?

Hebrews 5:7–9   *Jesus did not prove his love simply by following the rules, but by entering fully into his mission. It was through his prayers, and his obedience to the will of God that he brought salvation to all. His mission was his life, and through the fulfillment of this mission, he reached perfection.*

What Does This Example of Jesus Tell Me about Fulfilling My Mission in Life?

John 8:1–11   *Jesus did not come to condemn, but to forgive. He came to bring new life, while those who brought the adulterous woman to him were anxious to dwell on the faults of one's past life. Jesus concerned himself with forgiveness, while those who brought the woman sought condemnation for her. Jesus challenges them to look into their own hearts to see if they are innocent themselves. All leave quietly, and Jesus invites the woman to a new life of love.*

Am I Able to See the Good In Others and the Hope for the Future That Lives in Them, or Do I Easily Condemn Them for Their Past Faults?

Isaiah 43:16–21   *God offers new life and a new future to the Israelite nation. God does not remember the events of the past, but instead promises to bring new life for the future. The spirit of God is one of hope, and the aim of God's proclamation is that the chosen people will respond to this new hope by living up to the new life God offers them.*

How Does the Attitude of God in This Passage Challenge My Attitude toward Life?

Philippians 3:8–14   *Paul recognizes that all his successes come from the power of God working through him. He cannot stop in his mission to brag about his accomplishments, but he continues in the struggle, like a runner racing toward the finish line. He realizes that he has received blessings from the resurrection of Christ, and he implies that his readers should act as he does, using the gifts they have received while keeping their eyes on the true purpose of these gifts.*

How Well Am I Able to Balance My Use of the Gifts God Has Given to Me So That I May Show Concern for Others as Well as for Myself?

MY RESPONSE

Our attitude toward the gifts of Christ in our lives is important for God's plan of creation. God will always provide gifts, and God trusts us to use these gifts for the sake of others. Because of our gifts, we can spend our time proclaiming that we are better than others, or we can spend our time using our gifts for the good of God's creation.

In What Way Do I Intend to Use the Gifts I Have Received for the Good of God's Creation?

FURTHER DISCUSSION

1. How does Jesus' attitude toward new beginnings in life affect your daily life?

2. If you were to give a homily on Christ's attitude toward life, what examples from your own life would you give to explain Christ's message of new beginnings?

3. How can the message of new life help you as you begin to look toward the last two weeks of Lent?

PRAYER

Lord, Giver of Life,
you share with us the gifts of your resurrection.
Open our hearts to your life and your love,
that we might always live
the new life you promised
here and hereafter.
AMEN.

Passion Sunday

INTRODUCTION

With this Sunday, we begin Passion Week, the week in which we journey through the suffering and death of Jesus Christ and the meaning behind this suffering and death. Today's feast begins with triumph, the procession of Jesus into Jerusalem with crowds of people waving palm branches in honor and welcome. But immediately, we remember that Jesus has come into Jerusalem for "his hour," a time of confrontation with the powers of evil.

During this week, we realize what it means to be a follower of Christ. We meet a disciple who betrays Christ and does not repent and another who betrays and does repent. We meet a frightened Christ, tempted to call it all off, but accepting the will of God no matter what the cost. We meet a mob controlled by the influence of its leaders. We meet the ruler, Pilate, who is ruled by his own greed and fears.

In the midst of it all, we meet the suffering Jesus who can call out at his worst moment, "Father, forgive them, for they know not what they do."

This week is the moment of truth for the Christian. Now we must ask ourselves, Can we drink of the cup of suffering which Jesus has accepted for the sake of the world?

SCRIPTURE REFLECTIONS

Years A–B–C

(Year A) **Matthew 26:14–27:66 (or 27:11–54)**

(Year B) **Mark 14:1–15 (or 15:1–39)**

(Year C) **Luke 22:14–23:56 (or 23:1–49)**

The powerful God becomes powerless in this moment of darkness. God has chosen to give all power over to the domain of evil, but in the midst of this powerlessness, we discover the true meaning of power. Power consists in living out one's commitment to God and trusting in God. Evil seems to triumph, but defeat will soon follow. The message in our lives is that we are called to follow Jesus, to be willing to accept the powerlessness of our position in life to allow the power of God to manifest itself. On the surface, all seems lost. Only God and those who look back upon the event through the eyes of the resurrection see in this moment of defeat a moment of triumph for Jesus and for the world.

In What Ways Can I Apply the Passion to My Life as I Live It Today?

Isaiah 50:4–7   In the midst of suffering, the servant trusts in God, allowing himself to undergo physical and mental anguish, knowing that he will not be disgraced in the eyes of God. In this experience, the suffering servant is learning the meaning of trusting in God through all difficulty. The reading offers all people a hope in the strength and presence of God.

What Hope Does This Passage Offer Me in Moments of Suffering or Difficulty in My Life?

Philippians 2:6–11   *Jesus, as one with God, accepted our human frailty and continued to serve God in obedience, even unto death. Because of this great act of obedience and trust, God raised Jesus up to share in glory. Paul urges us to live with the same attitude. We could seek for glory, but the true path to holiness lies in following Jesus, in remaining obedient, even to death.*

How Can I Discover the Will of God in My Life, and How Am I Obedient to That Will?

MY RESPONSE

Someone once said that God will grant us our "Palm Sundays" before our "Good Fridays." This is another way of saying that God gives us comfort and strength to prepare us for the difficulties in our lives. The fact that the suffering of Jesus comes between his praise by the crowds on Palm Sunday and his resurrection from the dead reminds us that suffering is part of the journey through life, but it is not the total journey nor the goal of the journey. We are called to new life, even if it demands sacrifice or suffering to get there.

How Do I Intend to Apply the Message of the Passion to My Life?

FURTHER DISCUSSION

1. Some, looking at the passion of Jesus, believe that God calls us to a life of suffering. What do you think of this?

2. Citing examples from your own life, what would you say in a homily concerning the passion of Jesus?

3. How can you make the passion of Jesus a positive message for your life, rather than a negative one?

PRAYER

Lord, Our Suffering Servant,

you taught us the true worth
of suffering in obedience
to God's will.

Touch our minds and hearts
that we might see ourselves
as servants
responding to God's will
for the sake of others.

AMEN.

Holy Thursday

INTRODUCTION

The wonder of God begins to show itself even more brilliantly as we celebrate the gift of the Eucharist. Like a renowned designer planning the greatest event of the year, God has planned this gift from all eternity. On this day, we begin the sacred days of Holy Week.

SCRIPTURE REFLECTIONS

John 13:1–15   *At the peak moment of his life, before he passes to the Father, Jesus celebrates the Eucharistic Supper. Lest the disciples misunderstand the meaning of Jesus' life and their own call to be like Jesus, Jesus washes their feet and reminds them that they too are called to serve others. Before we enter into the full celebration of this Eucharistic meal, we too are reminded that a follower of Jesus is called to serve. As he has done, so should we do. Once we accept this attitude, we are ready for the celebration.*

What Does the Washing of the Feet by Jesus at the Last Supper Tell Me about the True Spirit of the Eucharist?

Exodus 12:1–8, 11–14   *This reading recalls the first passover meal, the celebration of the escape from slavery in Egypt. Just as God saved his people from the bonds of slavery in ancient times, so now Jesus will save his people from the bonds of sin and offer them a new Paschal meal. Just as the Jewish people saw in the Passover meal a moment of awe and miracle in history, so we should see our Eucharistic meal as the miraculous sign of God's love for his people.*

What Does the First Passover Tell Me about the Eucharist in Our Life?

1 Corinthians 11:23–26   *Paul presents the words and actions of Jesus at the Eucharistic meal. We are directed to perform this action in memory of Jesus, to make his life and death touch our world again.*

How Does My Share in the Spirit of the Eucharist Affect My Attitude toward Life?

142

PRAYER

(Write your own personal response.)

Good Friday

INTRODUCTION

The liturgy today leaves us with a sense of sadness and incompleteness. We end the liturgy in silence, and each family goes off to its own chores as the early followers of Jesus must have done after the burial. Christ has died! The day hangs heavily upon the world!

SCRIPTURE REFLECTIONS

John 18:1–19:42 *Through his death, Jesus draws the whole world to himself. Even at this moment when darkness seems to dominate, Jesus, the Light, has everything under control. In obedience to the Father, he allows himself to be led to death. The cross becomes the throne of Jesus, the king whose kingdom is not of this world. In accepting the call to Christianity and accepting the sacrifices necessary in living in union with Jesus, we too will draw all things to Jesus.*

What Is the Meaning of the Passion of Jesus for My Daily Life?

Isaiah 52:13–53:12   *This sight, so pitiable, points to Jesus who is God. He came as a servant, and offered himself with the meekness of a lamb being led to the slaughter. Those who did not know him would have considered him an evil person, getting the punishment he truly deserved. Those who did know him recognized that he died for the sins of many. Jesus, God, became the suffering servant!*

How Does This Passage from Isaiah the Prophet Offer Me Hope?

Hebrews 4:14–16, 5:7–9   *Jesus, the great High Priest now sharing in the glory of the resurrection, is no stranger to our struggles here on earth. Because he entered into our powerlessness to bring us salvation, he understands our weakness. Jesus is our model for endurance under suffering as well as the source of our salvation.*

What Does This Passage Tell Me about the Value of Being Weak in This World?

PRAYER

(Write your own personal response.)

Easter Joy—
A Private Session

INTRODUCTION

Out of darkness comes the light of Christ. On this most holy night, the Lord Jesus Christ passed from death to life in his resurrection. **This is the time for exultation!** We look back through the history of God's people and it all makes sense. God created the world, chose a family, led them from slavery to a new land, taught and shaped them in that new land, and chose this nation to give birth to the Messiah who has now been raised.

On this holy night, the community draws closer to Jesus as it welcomes others into the faithful, embracing them with the waters of baptism and their profession of faith, strengthening them through the oils of confirmation, and nourishing them through the gift of the Eucharist. The three Sacraments of Initiation into our Catholic Family highlight the celebration. For these gifts, Jesus has died, Jesus has been raised, the same Jesus will come again.

On this day, we celebrate the beginning of new life. On this day, we rejoice. **Jesus, our hope and our life, is raised from the dead!**

SCRIPTURE REFLECTIONS

Cycle A: **Matthew 28:1–10**

Cycle B: **Mark 16:1–85**

Cycle C: **Luke 24:1–12**

All the suffering and deprivation Jesus had to endure reaches its fulfillment in the resurrection. The gospel becomes truly the good news of Jesus Christ. A new day dawns, the first day of the week, when the fear of the

147

women and the other companions of Jesus turns to the joy of discovery and understanding. Jesus will meet them in Galilee, in the land of the Gentiles. Now, through the resurrection, the message of Jesus, the good news, will spread to the whole world.

What Message Do I Learn for My Daily Life from the Resurrection of Jesus?

Romans 6:3–11   The baptism into Christ is a commitment to Christ. Through baptism, we die with Christ to be raised with Christ. The concerns of the world should not control us as they would control a person with no hope in eternal life. We have died to sin through our baptism. We are free to grow closer to Christ. In Christ, through our baptism, we, like Christ, are **alive**!

In What Way Do the Sacraments of Initiation Help Me to Live My Life in Union with the Resurrected Christ?

MY RESPONSE

The message of Christ's resurrection became more meaningful to the disciples over a period of time. As they reflected upon the resurrection, they began to understand the total message of Jesus' life, death, and resurrection. Through the resurrection, they recognized that they were now called to spread the good news, a message of victory rather than a message of defeat. Their courage and joy became the great gifts which enabled them to spread the message of Jesus.

How Do I Intend to Live the Message of the Resurrection in My Daily Life?

PRAYER

(Write your own personal response.)

Rejoice in the Lord

INTRODUCTION

An elderly woman had died and left her coin collection to a favorite niece. At first the woman was enthusiastic about the inheritance until she found that her aunt had only thirty-five coins in her collection. One morning, many months later, she threw the coins into a bag and went off to work. During her lunch hour, she stopped at a coin shop to determine the value of the coins. Luckily, she chose a shop run by an honest and reputable coin dealer. When the man in the shop looked at the coins, he gasped in disbelief. These coins were extremely rare and extremely valuable. He brushed them off the counter and ushered the niece into his private office where he informed her of her great wealth. The niece admitted that she suspected the coins were of value, but she never suspected the extent of their value. These coins had remained on the top of a table in her bedroom for six months or more and had rested on the top of her desk all morning while she ran from one floor to the next engaged in her work. With the help of the shopkeeper, the woman was able to sell the coins for a large sum of money.

Our faith can be like the woman with these coins. Jesus left us with a great gift—his life. This life is given to us through our baptism and shared with us through the other sacraments. But we can leave this gift hanging around our lives, never really realizing its value. Now that we have celebrated the great feast of Easter, we must continue to consider the meaning of Easter in our lives as Christians.

During this session, we will seek to share our Easter joy with one another.

SCRIPTURE REFLECTIONS

Luke 24:1-12 *Sadness continually becomes joy for those who put their faith in Jesus. That is the theme of the Easter joy. Jesus died on the cross and a saddened group of women come to anoint his body. A new sadness overwhelms them at the sight of the empty tomb and the possibility of someone stealing the body of Jesus. But the message brings joy. Jesus is alive. The true believer must not look for the living among the dead, but must find in Jesus a living Christ who has conquered all the forces of evil and sin to bring us a new life. The good news of Christianity does not lie in the tomb but in resurrection.*

What Does This Passage Tell Me about the Message of Christ Which I Share as a Christian?

Philippians 4:4-7 *The Christian should be a person of great joy. Christ has died, Christ was raised, and Christ will come again. This is the great joy of Christianity, and this is the joy which should overflow into our lives. We should live in constant awareness of God's presence, trusting God unselfishly and praying often. When God becomes central to our lives, then we will begin to understand the full meaning of "Peace" wished so often throughout the Scriptures.*

How Has My Faith in Christ Affected My Attitude toward Life?

Colossians 3:1—4   *Once Christ touches our lives, we do not change in our external appearance, but we do experience the presence and faith of Christ within our lives. Our lives become hidden in Christ. All those very important needs for this life can begin to fade away under the light of Christ's resurrection and his gifts to us. Our glory in Christ is hidden now, but we shall see it clearly when God calls us to enter eternal life.*

What Does the Term "Peace" Mean to Me?

MY RESPONSE

Christ came to bring peace, but we soon learn that it is a special kind of peace. He does not call us to become timid or weak; he calls us to work for the peace of all people in the world. In working for peace, we can make people uncomfortable, especially those who feel that peace comes through violence or that peace means continually giving in. True peace comes through developing a firm faith in the message of Jesus and confronting the value of the world with the values of Christ. It comes with seeking a harmony between our lives and that of Christ, even if this harmony demands suffering and death as it did for Jesus. The resurrection reminds us that peace always wins in the end, and that we should devote ourselves to the peace of Christ.

How Do I Intend to Work for the Peace of Christ in the World?

FURTHER DISCUSSION

1. How do you feel about the fact that God has chosen to share the gift of faith with you?

2. What can you do as a member of the Catholic community to make the gifts of Christ more visible to the community?

3. What has the community done for you in strengthening your faith in Christ?

PRAYER

(Write your own personal response.)

Touching Wounds

INTRODUCTION

A family lost a six-month-old child through a sudden, unexplained death. The mother of the child continued her grieving for several months, not able to understand how God could let such a thing happen. None of her close friends could free this woman from her grief. One day, another woman, a stranger, stopped by the house and introduced herself as a mother who had lost a child under similar circumstances more than a year before. She shared her grief with the grieving mother, explaining how she worked her way through her own grief. After some time, the stranger left. For the first time since the child's death, the grieving mother arose from the chair she had used for many hours of weeping and began to prepare an elaborate dinner for her family. Through the wounds of another woman, she was able to accept her own wounds.

In becoming human, Jesus shared in our wounds. A spiritual writer by the name of Father Henri Nouwen wrote a book about Jesus entitled *The Wounded Healer.* Because Jesus shared our wounds, we trust his healing.

When we celebrate the resurrection of Jesus, we should never overlook his wounds. They are the signs of his glory. They remind us that his glory came through suffering, like our suffering, and that our wounds, like his, should lead us to our glory.

SCRIPTURE REFLECTIONS

John 20:19–31   *Jesus appeared to the disciples to share with them the great gifts of the Spirit. But Thomas was not present. In his grief, Thomas demanded the sign of the wounds of Jesus before he would believe. Jesus invited Thomas to touch those wounds and to believe in him.*

Because of the wounds, Thomas could call out to Jesus, "My Lord and my God!" If we really wish to understand the full glory of Christ's resurrection, we are to look to the wounds of Jesus and realize that in these wounds also lie the glory of Christ and our glory.

What Can I Learn from Christ about My Hurts and Wounds in Life?

Acts 2:42–47   The disciples of Jesus shared all they had with one another. Because of their willingness to proclaim Christ openly and to live with such love for one another, others joined them. These others may never have met Christ, but they found the image of Christ in his disciples.

What Does This Passage Tell Me about My Commitment to the Community?

1 Peter 1:3–12   *The author praises God for the new life which comes through baptism. He recognizes that baptism demands commitment, and at times this commitment could lead to suffering. But like gold that is tried by fire, so the true disciple proves himself or herself under difficult conditions. The author praises these disciples who have such great faith, despite the fact that they have never seen Christ.*

What Hope Can I Gain from This Passage?

MY RESPONSE

When we see people suffer, we wonder how a loving God could allow so much pain in the world. Through the Scriptures, we learn that we should touch the wounds of the world as Thomas touched the wounds of Christ, and that we should proclaim with Thomas, "My Lord and my God!" But this is difficult and it takes faith. The resurrection, by showing us that even suffering ends in victory, calls us to reach out with a loving touch to heal wounds in this world. Through touching the wounds of the world with faith, we bring about healing.

How Do I Intend to Touch the Wounds of the World?

FURTHER DISCUSSION

1. Do you think it important that an image of the resurrected Christ carry the sign of his wounds?

2. Should a Christian seek to suffer as much as she or he can endure?

3. Does the image of the suffering of Jesus make Christianity a sad religion?

PRAYER

(Write your own personal response.)

Jesus the Stranger

INTRODUCTION

We walk with Christ every moment of our day. The problem is that we are so often taken up with our own duties, our own sadness and our own pleasures that we fail to take notice of Christ who journeys along with us. For the Catholic, the celebration of the Eucharist is a time to pause and to recognize in the stranger, who walks along with us, the presence of Christ.

Jesus has been raised and Jesus is alive in the world. But he looks very different. He is in the woman weeping over a dead husband, the man slouched along the sidewalk beside an empty whiskey bottle, the boy and girl laughing on a swing in a park, and the workers who rush off in the brisk morning air to their jobs. Once we recognize Christ in the stranger, we feel our hearts burning within us.

Once we discover Christ in the world, we cannot rest. We rush off to share the message, to tell others the good news. Many will tell us that they have already discovered the fact that Christ is alive, while others will laugh at the naive thought that Christ walks with us.

But Christ is here, with us on our journey, leading us to the door of his home where we will recognize him "in the breaking of the bread."

SCRIPTURE REFLECTIONS

Luke 24:13–35   *The two disciples had followed Christ for some days during his public life. They had hoped in him, but now he has died as a common criminal. Christ, the stranger who walks with them, reminds them of a journey which the Messiah must make in order to enter into his glory. He must go through his passover experience as the Old*

Testament had foretold. The disciples were learning how to read the Old Testament through the eyes of the resurrection. Their hearts begin to warm within them, but they pay no attention. They listen to the stranger! Finally, in the breaking of the bread, the Eucharist, they recognize the risen Christ, and their sorrow melts into joy.

What Does This Passage Say Concerning My Journey as a Christian?

Acts 2:14, 22–28   On Pentecost, Peter faced the crowd with the courage of a man drunk with faith in Christ and hope through the Spirit. For three years he had spent time with Jesus. Now that he understood the resurrection of Jesus, he understood Christ. It was as though he had spent three years with a stranger, never fully grasping the depth of the person he called "Master." Peter now told the crowd about the friend he loved so dearly. This friend had performed many miracles. He had also been put to death at the urging of the Israelite leaders and at the hands of the pagan army. But he was raised. David had spoken of Jesus so many centuries before, stating that God would never allow the corruption of death to touch this chosen one. Now, through the resurrection of Jesus, Peter could understand the message of David. Peter wanted the crowd to recognize Christ as he had recognized him.

What Does This Passage Tell Me about My Need to Share the Message of Jesus?

1 Peter 1:17–21 *Like Christ, the disciple must pass through death to enter into glory. The life the Christian lives and shares in at this time is a pilgrimage, a journey toward a life of glory and happiness with Jesus. Through the death and resurrection of Christ, the true goal and meaning of our own journey becomes visible. Looking to the whole of Jesus' life and message, we realize that our life and death are the pathways to our resurrection and to our glory. It is from Jesus' life and message that we learn the meaning of our life.*

What Does This Passage Tell Me about My Life in Christ?

MY RESPONSE

Throughout our lives, Christ is present to us without our recognizing him. We meet him in our relatives, friends, acquaintances, people who brush past us in the street and in the dying people of our countries. We are like the disciples on the road to Emmaus. We meet Christ in our friends and enemies, and when we take time out to celebrate the Eucharist, we can suddenly become aware of Christ's presence in our world. The Eucharist is meant to help us look at the many ways Christ comes to us in the world, and to help us recognize him "in the breaking of the bread." With this faith, we, as Christians, must face the world with joy and hope, because we recognize through our lives that Jesus the Lord is truly risen and living.

How Do I Intend to Make Use of My Belief That I Can Experience the Presence of Christ with Every Person I Meet?

FURTHER DISCUSSION

1. What can we do to deepen our awareness of God's presence in all people around us?

2. Is our life any different because we have been baptized?

3. How can we, too, recognize Christ "in the breaking of the bread"?

PRAYER

(Write your own personal response.)

Sharing Christ

INTRODUCTION

A crippled man, frustrated by the problems he encountered in public buildings whenever he had to push his wheelchair into elevators, down halls, or into rest rooms, decided that he would make the State Legislature conscious of his problem and perhaps correct it in some way. But he faced a further problem. The State House itself was not made for people who are disabled. The man wrote to a friend concerned about people with disabilities and asked him, "Will you be my feet?" Through the efforts of this friend, much has been done to raise the consciousness of people concerning the needs of the disabled for simple movement in a busy world.

In God's plan, Christ entered our human family and shared his life and message with us. But Christ, being human, had to face the fact that men and women die or are killed within a certain number of years. Jesus had to face death once he accepted our humanness. But God had further plans. When Jesus died, was raised, and ascended, he looked to us and asked, "Will you be my feet and my voice?" In our baptism, we say "Yes."

SCRIPTURE REFLECTIONS

Mark 16:9–20   *Jesus revealed himself to many, but the Eleven refused to accept the testimony of others. Finally, Jesus appeared to them while they were at the table. The imagery of the table here suggests the celebration of the Eucharist. In Mark's Gospel, Jesus gives the Eleven a special mission at this time to carry out their call as disciples, to trust in Jesus, baptize in his name, and perform great acts in his name. He points to their need for faith before he departs from their midst.*

How Well Prepared Am I to Carry Out My Mission as a Christian?

Matthew 28:16–20   *Jesus proclaims that he has full authority in heaven and on earth and that he will share this with his disciples. He orders them to go out to all peoples, to teach them and to baptize them and to trust in the fact that he is always with them.*

How Does My Awareness of Christ's Presence In My Life Help Me in the Fulfillment of My Mission to Share the Message of Christ with Others?

163

Acts 1:1–11   *As the disciples watch Jesus being taken up to heaven, two men in white direct them toward their mission. They are not to stand there "looking up," but to spread Christ's message to all the world. Jesus will come again, but in the meanwhile, they have a mission to perform.*

What Is the Message of the Ascension for My Life?

MY RESPONSE

If we spend our lives in prayer while at the same time ignoring the needs of the people of the world, we could be like the disciples who "stand looking up." Our call is to learn from the message of Christ how to live as a Christian and to live as Christ would have us live. It is a life of prayer and one of concern for the world in which we live. We cannot escape from our world, even in prayer, and all our needs and the needs of the world demand our time, our energy, and our prayers.

How Do I Intend to Share the Message of Christ Which I Have Received?

FURTHER DISCUSSION

1. How can we share the person and message of Jesus Christ in our lives today?

2. Is it possible for us to expect to make any changes in the world?

3. What are some of the things we must avoid if we do not wish to become complacent Christians?

PRAYER

(Write your own personal response.)

Christ Will Come Again

INTRODUCTION

The end of the world was coming! The signs of the book of Revelation were unmistakably seen in the world. Men, women and children, doctors, lawyers, laborers and the unemployed sold all that they had to go to the mountain to meet the Lord in his second coming. As foolish as this might sound, it happened a few years back! And the world did not end!

There is something about the end of the world that fascinates people and drives them into a frenzy. Many fear being alive on that great day when the Lord comes while others long to be alive on that day.

When the time for the end of the world does come, our concern should be that we have done our part to make the world ready. God does not want us to panic because we think the world will end tomorrow, but God would like us to love our brothers and sisters as though that were the fact. We should be ready . . . always. And, we should see this great day as a day of rejoicing when Christ comes to claim his creation for God.

SCRIPTURE REFLECTIONS

Matthew 24:36–51   *No one knows when the world will end. Jesus tells us that life will be going on that day as it had in the past. God is not saying that people will or will not be doing wrong on that day. Life will be normal when the world ends and God comes to take the good into eternal life. Jesus tells a parable which praises the servants who live every day well-prepared for the master's return. But the parable has a harsh lesson for those who think there will be sufficient warning to correct faults before the end. We must always be alert in the Lord, because we do not know the day nor the hour.*

What Message for My Life Can I Learn from This Passage?

1 Thessalonians 4:13–18   The people of the early Church were so excited about the thought of the second coming of Christ that they feared for those who died before this event took place. Paul had to assure them that even those who had died would share in the great gifts of the Lord. After the death, resurrection, and ascension of Jesus, the early Church thought that the second coming of Christ was not far off. From our vantage point of two thousand years later, we can see how wrong the members of the early Church were when they tried to guess the time of the second coming. They do, however, teach us that the day of the second coming should be one of joy rather than one of dread.

Am I Able to Feel Joy At the Thought of the Second Coming of Christ?

Revelation 22:12–17   *Christ is coming soon to take us all into a life of eternal happiness with him. He was existing from the beginning and he will be there at the end. For those robed in the white garment of faithfulness, a new garden of paradise will begin. They will discover the real joy and meaning of the "tree of life." For those who thirst for love and the peace of Christ, the invitation goes out to them from Christ. With the thought in mind that we will meet Christ and be brought into his heavenly home, we should really long to be with "the Morning Star" which shines with such a brilliance of love.*

In What Way Do My Thoughts about an Eternal Reward Help Me in This Life?

MY RESPONSE

We must all face death. Whether the world ends, or our life ends before the world ends, does not really matter to many of us. We are all called to resurrection. We can look at our lives as so many years during which we put in time and energy and then unfairly die, or we can see our lives as an opportunity for building up God's creation. For those who use their talents and gifts well, the moment of death is a moment of triumph, a time when we rejoice that Christ is coming again for us. Death adds an urgency to life, and the coming of Christ reminds us that death can be victorious.

How Do I Intend to Make My Life Meaningful for God?

FURTHER DISCUSSION

1. How do you picture the end of the world? Would you welcome it?

2. Why are people so willing to listen to predictions of the end of the world and even act upon them?

3. The Gospels are called the "good news." Looking back over the Gospels and the message of the New Testament, how could you say that this is the good news right down to the end?

PRAYER

(Write your own personal response.)

Session Number _____

Date _____

Pentecost: The Holy Spirit among Us

INTRODUCTION

A war hero once told a group of students that, with a gun in his hand, he was willing to face any enemy. But without a gun, he had a great fear of facing an enemy. A few years earlier, a friend had asked him to take part in a nonviolent demonstration against some city planners who were evicting poor people from their homes without offering them any alternative for housing. Without his gun to protect him, the man suddenly felt weak and vulnerable as he faced an army of equally-reluctant police who had the unhappy duty of breaking up the demonstration. That day he was kicked and dragged through the streets, but he felt strangely satisfied when the demonstration yielded results and the city planners found alternative housing for the poor. He recognized that there was a power in life greater than the power of weapons.

On the Feast of Pentecost, we celebrate the presence of a great power in our lives in the person of the Holy Spirit. Through the power of the Spirit, the Church dares to confront the power of evil in the world, knowing that evil can be overcome by the power of God's love. Pentecost is a feast which reminds us that God continues to live in the world through God's people and that, with such a loving force—the power of the Spirit—we can continue to live in hope for a better world.

SCRIPTURE REFLECTION

John 20:19–23   *In this reading, Jesus offers his disciples a new power. He breathes on them and invites them to receive the Holy Spirit. The forgiveness of sins Jesus mentioned in this passage includes not only the doing away* with the sins, but also the entrance into a new life. Jesus is telling the disciples that they now have the power to go out and invite others to a share in salvation, to bring them to a life of forgiveness and love through baptism.

How Does the Holy Spirit Guide Me in My Sharing of the Love of Christ?

Genesis 11:1–9   In the days when the storyteller told about the tower builders, the Israelites had become accustomed to large towers at the entrance of major cities. During their captivity in Babylon, they discovered a huge tower built by people whose language they did not understand. The message behind the story of the building of the tower of Babel is one of disruption of God's creation. As long as people followed the message of God, they would reach heaven. If they tried to reach paradise through their own sinful ways, they would find frustration and alienation in this world. The mission of the Holy Spirit is to help people work together once again, not by making us all speak the same language, but by enabling us to live together in a common experience of compassion, love and caring.

How Does the Story of the Building of the Tower of Babel Help Me to Understand the Need for the Holy Spirit in My Life?

Romans 8:22–27   *Jesus came to bring salvation to the world. If Jesus did this, then why is the world the same? Why is sin so strong? Why did Jesus not change the world by his life so that sin was no longer powerful? Paul answers these questions by reminding us that creation has not reached its final goal. It is still "groaning" toward this end, and we are the ones who complete the fullness of salvation brought by Jesus. To do this, we need the power and the spirit Jesus had. We need the Holy Spirit. The Spirit of Jesus brings us this power.*

What Encouragement Can I Take from the Fact That the Holy Spirit Is Continually Guiding Me?

MY RESPONSE

Throughout the reflections in this book, we learned that God expects much from Christians. We live in a world created by God, a world which demands respect simply because it has God as its source. In this world, we face the challenge of discovering the presence of God as we choose to love our families, our friends, and even our enemies. The love demanded aims to lift us above the selfish allurements of our lives and to raise us to a fuller life in union with God. In a sense, we are called to live in this world with the recognition that it is the beginning of our eternity, that we will now live forever. The life of love which we will now live forever should begin here in this world and never end. The goal seems impossible, yet with the help of the Holy Spirit, we can do the impossible. With the Holy Spirit, we can perform great deeds for God. This is not simply the goal of our life on earth, but the goal of our eternal life, and the Spirit helps us to begin it now.

How Do I Intend to Become More Conscious of the Mission of the Holy Spirit in My Life?

FURTHER DISCUSSION

1. What are some ways in which the Holy Spirit helps you throughout your daily life?

2. Give an example from your own life, or the life of someone you know, which you would consider an example of the activity of the Holy Spirit in our world.

3. What gift of the Holy Spirit would you consider most important for your life?

PRAYER

Come, Holy Spirit,
Fill us with an awareness of your presence.
Guide us with your wisdom,
and inspire us with your love.
AMEN.

APPENDIX I

The themes found in the reflections for the Easter Season follow the themes developed in the season itself rather than the readings from cycles A, B, and C for each of the Sundays. To add reflections for each of these cycles would have come close to doubling the size of this book. For those who wish to follow the Sunday readings for the Easter Season as well as for those who wish to reflect on significant feasts and liturgies, we have listed here the readings for these feasts.

EASTER VIGIL

Nine readings are assigned to the Easter Vigil. Seven are from the Old Testament and two from the New Testament. This chapter reflects on the two New Testament readings. Those who wish to reflect on some or all of the Old Testament readings will find them in their Bible as follows:

(A-B-C) Genesis 1:1–2:2; Genesis 22:1–18; Exodus 14:15–15:1; Isaiah 54:5–14; Isaiah 55:1–11; Baruch 3:9–15; 32–4:4; Ezekiel 36:16–28.

SUNDAYS OF EASTER

Easter Sunday (A-B-C) Acts 10:34, 37–43; Colossians 3:1–4 or 1 Corinthians 5:6–8; John 20:1–9.

Second Sunday (A) Acts 2:42–47; 1 Peter 1:3–9; John 20:19–31.
(B) Acts 4:32–35; 1 John 5:1–6; John 20:19–31.
(C) Acts 5:12–16; Revelation 1:9–13, 17–19; John 20:19–31.

Third Sunday (A) Acts 2:14, 22–28; 1 Peter 1:17–21; Luke 24:13–35.
(B) Acts 3:13–15, 17–19; 1 John 2:1–5; Luke 24:35–48.
(C) Acts 5:27–32, 40–41; Revelation 5:11–14; John 21:1–19 or John 21:1–14.

Fourth Sunday (A) Acts 2:14, 36–41; 1 Peter 2:20–25; John 10:1–10.
(B) Acts 4:8–12; 1 John 3:1–2; John 10:11–18.
(C) Acts 13:14, 43–52; Revelation 7:9, 14–17; John 10:27–30.

Fifth Sunday (A) Acts 6:1–7; 1 Peter 2:4–9; John 14:1–12.
(B) Acts 9:26–31; 1 John 3:18–24; John 15:1–8.
(C) Acts 14:21–27; Revelation 21:1–5; John 13:31–35.

Sixth Sunday (A) Acts 8:5–8, 14–17; 1 Peter 3:15–18; John 14:15–21.
(B) Acts 10:25–26, 34–35, 44–48; 1 John 4:7–10; John 15:9–17.
(C) Acts 15:1–2, 22–29; Revelation 21:10–14, 22–23; John 14:23–29.

Seventh Sunday (A) Acts 1:12–14; 1 Peter 4:13–16; John 17:1–11.
(B) Acts 1:15–17, 20–26; 1 John 4:11–16; John 17:11–19.
(C) Acts 7:55–60; Revelation 22:12–14, 16–17, 20; John 17:20–26.

VIGIL OF PENTECOST

(A-B-C) Genesis 11:1–9 or Exodus 19:3–8, 16–20 or Ezekiel 37:1–14 or Joel 3:1–5; Romans 8:22–27; John 7:37–39.

PENTECOST SUNDAY

(A-B-C) Acts 2:1–11; 1 Corinthians 12:3–7, 12–13; John 20:19–23.

ASCENSION

(A-B-C) Acts 1:1–11; Ephesians 1:17–23; Matthew 28:16–20 (A), Mark 16:15–20 (B), Luke 24:46–53 (C).

CHRISTMAS

Vigil (A-B-C) Isaiah 62:1–5; Acts 13:16–17, 22–25; Matthew 1:1–25 or 1:18–25.

Midnight (A-B-C) Isaiah 9:1–6; Titus 2:11–14; Luke 2:1–14.

Dawn (A-B-C) Isaiah 62:11–12; Titus 3:4–7; Luke 2:15–20.

Day (A-B-C) Isaiah 52:7–10; Hebrews 1:1–6; John 1:1–18 or 1–5, 9–14.

APPENDIX II

Table of Principal Celebrations of the Liturgical Year

Year	Sunday Cycle	Weekday Cycle	Epiphany	Baptism of the Lord	Ash Wednesday	Easter	Ascension
1987	A	I	4 Jan.	11 Jan.	4 Mar.	19 Apr.	28 May
1988	B	II	3 Jan.	10 Jan.	17 Feb.	3 Apr.	12 May
1989	C	I	8 Jan.	9 Jan.	8 Feb.	26 Mar.	4 May
1990	A	II	7 Jan.	8 Jan.	28 Feb.	15 Apr.	24 May
1991	B	I	6 Jan.	13 Jan.	13 Feb.	31 Mar.	9 May
1992	C	II	5 Jan.	12 Jan.	4 Mar.	19 Apr.	28 May
1993	A	I	3 Jan.	10 Jan.	24 Feb.	11 Apr.	20 May
1994	B	II	2 Jan.	9 Jan.	16 Feb.	3 Apr.	12 May
1995	C	I	8 Jan.	9 Jan.	1 Mar.	16 Apr.	25 May
1996	A	II	7 Jan.	8 Jan.	21 Feb.	7 Apr.	16 May
1997	B	I	5 Jan.	12 Jan.	12 Feb.	30 Mar.	8 May
1998	C	II	4 Jan.	11 Jan.	25 Feb.	12 Apr.	21 May
1999	A	I	3 Jan.	10 Jan.	17 Feb.	4 Apr.	13 May
2000	B	II	2 Jan.	9 Jan.	8 Mar.	23 Apr.	1 June
2001	C	I	7 Jan.	8 Jan.	28 Feb.	15 Apr.	24 May
2002	A	II	6 Jan.	13 Jan.	20 Feb.	7 Apr.	16 May
2003	B	I	5 Jan.	12 Jan.	12 Feb.	30 Mar.	8 May
2004	C	II	4 Jan.	11 Jan.	3 Mar.	18 Apr.	27 May
2005	A	I	2 Jan.	9 Jan.	16 Feb.	3 Apr.	12 May
2006	B	II	8 Jan.	9 Jan.	8 Feb.	26 Mar.	4 May
2007	C	I	7 Jan.	8 Jan.	28 Feb.	15 Apr.	24 May
2008	A	II	6 Jan.	13 Jan.	20 Feb.	6 Apr.	15 May
2009	B	I	4 Jan.	11 Jan.	4 Mar.	19 Apr.	28 May
2010	C	II	3 Jan.	10 Jan.	24 Feb.	11 Apr.	20 May

Weeks in Ordinary Time

		before Lent		after Easter Season		
Pentecost	The Body and Blood of Christ	Number of weeks	Ending	Beginning	In week number	First Sunday of Advent
7 June	21 June	8	3 Mar.	8 June	10	29 Nov.
22 May	5 June	6	16 Feb.	23 May	8	27 Nov.
14 May	28 May	5	7 Feb.	15 May	6	3 Dec.
3 June	17 June	8	27 Feb.	4 June	9	2 Dec.
19 May	2 June	5	12 Feb.	20 May	7	1 Dec.
7 June	21 June	8	3 Mar.	8 June	10	29 Nov.
30 May	13 June	7	23 Feb.	31 May	9	28 Nov.
22 May	5 June	6	15 Feb.	23 May	8	27 Nov.
4 June	18 June	8	28 Feb.	5 June	9	3 Dec.
26 May	9 June	7	20 Feb.	27 May	8	1 Dec.
18 May	1 June	5	11 Feb.	19 May	7	30 Nov.
31 May	14 June	7	24 Feb.	1 June	9	29 Nov.
23 May	6 June	6	16 Feb.	24 May	8	28 Nov.
11 June	25 June	9	7 Mar.	12 June	10	3 Dec.
3 June	17 June	8	27 Feb.	4 June	9	2 Dec.
26 May	9 June	6	19 Feb.	27 May	8	1 Dec.
18 May	1 June	5	11 Feb.	19 May	7	30 Nov.
6 June	20 June	8	2 Mar.	7 June	10	28 Nov.
22 May	5 June	6	15 Feb.	23 May	8	27 Nov.
14 May	28 May	5	7 Feb.	15 May	6	3 Dec.
3 June	17 June	8	27 Feb.	4 June	9	2 Dec.
25 May	8 June	6	19 Feb.	26 May	8	30 Nov.
7 June	21 June	8	3 Mar.	8 June	10	29 Nov.
30 May	13 June	7	23 Feb.	31 May	9	28 Nov.

Other Books by Rev. William A. Anderson

In His Light

A major resource for the RCIA, this 1986 revised catechism presents the what and why of Catholic doctrine regarding God, Jesus, sin, sacraments, death, and much more. Scripture texts and allegorical stories help illustrate the basics of Catholicism. Included are the latest thoughts and trends which show the contemporary Church in action. By Rev. William A. Anderson.

RCIA: A Total Parish Process

Subtitled "How to Implement the RCIA in Your Parish," this new resource offers suggestions which can be used for further adaptations in the RCIA process. Using the RCIA as a source of renewal for the entire parish family, the book outlines ways for teaching, training, experiencing, sharing, and motivating. Written by Rev. William A. Anderson.

Journeying with Christ

This series of books, each on a different topic, offers adults the opportunity to reflect on the Scripture, the teachings of Christ and the Church, and stories of faith.

Each book in the series follows the same basic format and has the following features: stories, information, Scripture, personal decisions, and discussion. Written by Rev. William A. Anderson, the books can be used by individuals or groups.

Journeying through the RCIA

A journey to help adults understand what the RCIA can mean to both the parish community and to individuals within the community.

Journeying toward Baptism

A journey of preparing for Baptism by reflecting on the unique and personal experience of the birth, the family, the child, the religious community, and the sacrament itself.

Journeying toward Marriage

A journey reflecting on the couple's relationship and the sacrament of marriage as a lifetime commitment.

Other RCIA Resources

Step-by-Step: A Catechetical Handbook for the RCIA

For parishes just beginning to integrate the RCIA into the whole complex of parish life, this new resource provides all the tools needed to ensure a successful program. For each of the four stages it offers session outlines and resource articles that give practical direction and encouragement.
Written by Mary T. Malone.

RCIA: Foundations of Christian Initiation

Providing a general introduction to Christian Initiation as well as guidelines and starters for its implementation is the focus of this reference. The book covers the different stages of initiation, its history, and the special issues regarding initiation. Commissioned by the Archdiocese of Dubuque, Office of Religious Education.

RCIA: A Practical Approach to Christian Initiation

To help restore the catechumenate structure, this book offers a complete guide for implementing the RCIA. It provides program sessions, worksheets, outlines for the rites, and guidelines for facilitating the program. Written by a five-member ministry team.